THE MCDONALDS OF LANSINGBURGH, RENSSELAER COUNTY, NEW YORK

The Pioneering Family of Richard and Catharine (Lansing) McDonald and Their Descendants

A supplemental addition to
A Revolutionary American Family:
The McDonalds of Somerset County, New Jersey,
affirming the relationship of Richard McDonald
of Lansingburgh to Maj. Richard McDonald of
Pluckemin and Bedminster, New Jersey

by Laurence Overmire

Indelible Mark Publishing
West Linn, OR

Enumerating the families of
Richard L. McDonald,
Catharine McDonald Adams and
Elizabeth McDonald Wells

Featuring McDonald/MacDonald families of
Albany County, New York, and Lake Dallas, Texas,
as well as many interrelated and descendant families

And including interrelated families: Ackley, Adams, Augustine,
Baker, Calden, Collard, DeLamater, Gale, Goodwin, Harlow,
Hun, Kelley, Kerr, Ladewig, Lang, Lansing, MacAdams, Main,
Marsland, McAllen, McCurley, Miles, Miller, Morris, Peltz, Ransom,
Robinson, Russell, Schmidt, Siek, Smith, Stapf, Tucker, Turner,
Unger, Van Arnum, Wahlstrom, Wells, White, Williams
and many more.

Indelible Mark Publishing 2021

Copyright © 2021 by Laurence Overmire

Library of Congress Control Number: 2020951294

ISBN 978-1-7349408-2-4

Front cover photo: American militia at reenactment of the Battle of Bound Brook,
Abraham Staats House in South Bound Brook, NJ *(photo by Jody Gibian-Miles, 2014)*

Back cover photo: Author Laurence Overmire kneels by the grave of Maj. Richard McDonald
at the Old Somerville Cemetery in Somerville, NJ *(photo by Nancy McDonald, 2014)*

Book design and editing by Nancy McDonald

INDELIBLE MARK PUBLISHING, LLC
6498 Lowry Drive, # 4
West Linn, OR 97068
www.indeliblemarkpublishing.com

DEDICATION

For Michael John McDonald (1939-2020) whose keen desire
to know his McDonald forbears inspired us to learn more and more
about the McDonalds of Somerset County, New Jersey and their descendants.

ALSO BY LAURENCE OVERMIRE

BOOKS

William R. McDonald and Abigail Fowler of Herkimer County, New York
and Their Descendants

The One Idea That Saves The World (2nd edition)
A Message of Hope in a Time of Crisis

Digging for Ancestral Gold
The Fun and Easy Way to Get Started on Your Genealogy Quest

A Revolutionary American Family
The McDonalds of Somerset County, New Jersey

The One Idea That Saves The World (1st edition)
A Call to Conscience and A Call to Action

One Immigrant's Legacy
The Overmyer Family in America, 1751-2009

POETRY BOOKS

New York Minute
An Actor's Memoir

The Ghost of Rabbie Burns
An American Poet's Journey Through Scotland

Gone Hollywood

Report From X-Star 10
Sci-Fi Poetry

Honor & Remembrance
A Poetic Journey through American History

Visit the author at:

laurenceovermire.com
facebook.com/poet.laurence.overmire

CONTENTS

INTRODUCTION

Genealogy is an ongoing process and requires periodic updating.

Shortly after we published *A Revolutionary American Family: The McDonalds of Somerset County, New Jersey* (May 29, 2015), another potential branch of the McDonalds came to our attention, the line of William R. McDonald, the eldest son of Revolutionary War veteran, Maj. Richard McDonald of Somerset County. After months of research that line was confirmed to be authentic. The results were published in *William R. McDonald and Abigail Fowler of Herkimer County, New York* (Indelible Mark Publishing, 2015).

While completing that second book, another unknown line of the McDonalds of Somerset County, New Jersey, was discovered: the line of Richard McDonald, second son of Maj. Richard McDonald of Somerset County. He was the younger brother of William R. McDonald. His family is the subject of this book.

Richard McDonald's family has never been detailed before. It represents a branch of the McDonald tree that has been completely lost until now.

This all came about thanks to the name Richard gave his son: Lansing McDonald. Quite accidentally, we came across some guardianship papers in Somerset County, New Jersey, that showed Lansing McDonald, a minor, had requested George McDonald become his guardian. The papers were signed with the distinctive signature of George McDonald, aka Col. George McDonald, the famous lawyer who eventually moved to Vincennes, Indiana, and became part of the legal team there that argued to abolish slavery before the Indiana Supreme Court. Samuel Swan, George's brother-in-law, who became a U.S. Representative, also signed the papers.

Somerset County, New Jersey
by David Benbennick

After more in-depth research it became clear that Col. George McDonald was Lansing's uncle, the younger brother of his father, Richard McDonald of Lansingburgh, New York.

Unfortunately, because no previous genealogy has been recorded on the early roots of this family, some of the descendant branches remain unknown. Though many modern-day descendants of Richard and Catharine (Lansing) McDonald have been discovered, very few of them still carry the surname McDonald. In fact, the only McDonalds in this branch of the tree known to be alive today are the descendants of Richard Earl MacDonald (1894-1980). It would be most helpful if one or more of those descendants would take a Y-DNA test to further confirm the ancestral line.

As always, we recommend that male McDonalds who would like to identify their McDonald lineage join the Clan Donald USA Genetic Genealogy Project and have their Y-DNA tested. The more McDonalds who take the test, the easier it will be for McDonalds all over the world to determine how they are related to Clan Donald.

This book, however, represents only one small branch of the extensive McDonald family tree that took root in Somerset County, New Jersey. The rest of the history, the fascinating origins of this family dating back to 1685, and the progenitors who brought it into being, are discussed in their entirety in *A Revolutionary American Family: The McDonalds of Somerset County, New Jersey*. This volume is but an addendum to that much larger work.

Now sit down, get comfortable, perhaps grab a cup of coffee, a cup of tea, or another favorite beverage and relax. You are about to meet Richard and Catharine (Lansing) McDonald of Lansingburgh, Rensselaer County, New York, and read the fascinating stories of their descendants who have made their homes in communities all across this great nation of ours, the United States of America.

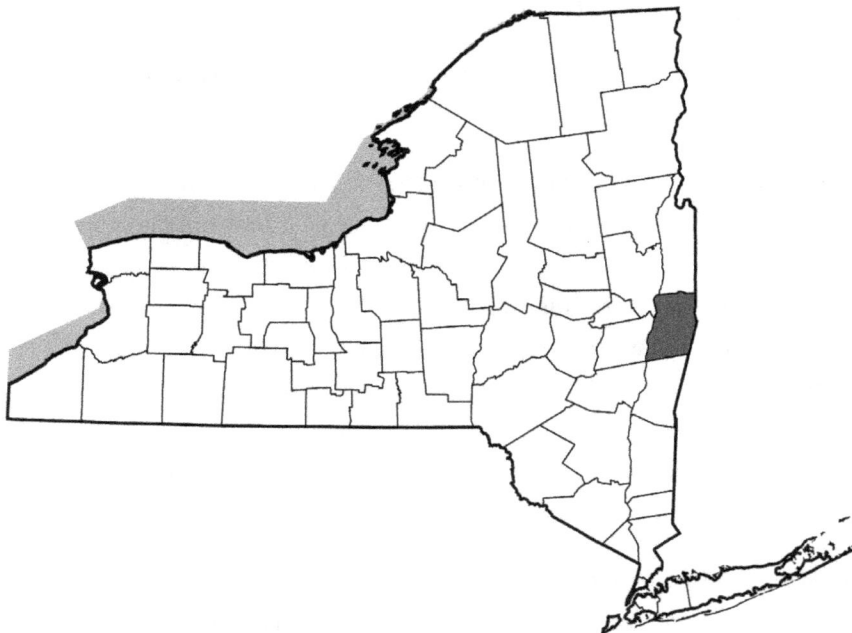

Rensselaer County, New York
by David Benbennick

Chapter 1

RICHARD AND CATHARINE (LANSING) MCDONALD
of Lansingburgh, New York

Great Grandparents: William and Florance MacDonel
Grandparents: Col. William McDonald and Unknown First Wife
Parents: Maj. Richard McDonald and Margrietje Schamp
Siblings: William R., Phebe, George, Sarah

RICHARD MCDONALD (c. 1762-1812)
+ Catharine Lansing (c. 1768-1812)

1. Richard L. McDonald (c. 1789-c. 1869, m. Sophia Van Arnum, Susan Rowley)
2. Catharine McDonald (c. 1790-aft 1818, m. James Adams)
3. Abraham McDonald (c. 1791-aft. 1836, m. Unknown)
4. Lansing McDonald (c. 1796-aft. 1836)
5. Elizabeth McDonald (c. 1800-1872, m. Philander Wells)
6. Alanson McDonald (1802-bef 1829)
7. Jane McDonald (c. 1803-1834)
8. George McDonald (1808-aft. 1844)
9. Jacob McDonald (c. 1809-aft. 1844)

Richard McDonald, we now know, was the second-born son and namesake of Revolutionary War hero, Maj. Richard McDonald, who served with distinction in the First Somerset New Jersey militia in the Revolutionary War under Col. Frederick Frelinghuysen. Maj. Richard no doubt knew Gen. George Washington personally. The fascinating details of his life and times and that of his influential family have been documented previously in *A Revolutionary American Family: The McDonalds of Somerset County, New Jersey*.[1]

The younger Richard and his family, however, have been a complete mystery until now. Their story has never before been recorded. Nothing about them is known to have been passed down to their descendants to this day. What we have discovered has been painstakingly gleaned from the few available records that have survived the test of time.

Previously, we knew from Maj. Richard's will that he had a son named Richard who had children. Those children inherited part of the estate, but were not identified by name. Richard himself was assumed to have died sometime before 1820 when his father wrote the will. His birth date had been approximated at 1773,[2] but that's about all that was known of him.

We now know that Richard McDonald must have been born about 1762,[3] probably in Bedminster, Somerset County, New Jersey. He was about a year younger than his brother William R. and about six years older than brother George, who would grow up to become the famous lawyer who died tragically in Indiana in 1820.

The boys and their two sisters, Phebe and Sarah, would have grown up in the midst of the American Revolution. Their mother, Margrietje Schamp McDonald, died young at age 35 just before the Revolution began in the summer of 1773. The family probably attended the Reformed Dutch Church with which their mother was associated through her parents, Joost "George" and Kniertje (Montfoort) Schamp. Joost died before the children were born. Kniertje lived until 1771, so she would have been able to spend at least some time with her grandchildren before she died. Margrietje Schamp McDonald was buried in the Bedminster Reformed Church Cemetery. Her son, Richard McDonald, was only about 11 years old.

Soon after his wife died, Maj. Richard took a second wife. After all, his children needed a mother. Her name was Catharine Rosbrugh McCrea, the widow of Rev. James McCrea, pastor of the Lamington Presbyterian Church near Pluckemin, New Jersey. Catharine was, of course, a leading member of the Lamington congregation, so the McDonalds quickly became prominent members there as well.

Catharine also must have brought her own children to the McDonald household: Philip, Creighton and Catherine McCrea, all of whom were fairly close in age to Richard. Catharine's eldest child, Robert, was about 20 years old. He may have stayed with the McDonalds initially, but soon he would enlist in the British army to fight against the Americans, his own kin, in the Revolution. He rose to the rank of major and was severely wounded at the Battle of Brandywine in 1777.[4] After the war, it is said, he became Governor of the Channel Islands in Britain.[5]

Catharine's second son, Philip McCrea, enlisted as a sergeant with the American Continental Army and was promoted to the rank of lieutenant. On June 2, 1781, while strolling down the street in Elizabethtown, New Jersey, with his brother-in-law David Woodruff, he was halted by a sentinel. Apparently, Philip didn't answer the soldier immediately. Perhaps he was engrossed in conversation. Whatever the delay, those few split seconds cost him his life. The apprehensive sentinel pulled the trigger and shot him dead.[6]

The American Revolution was a trying time for all those who lived through it. The McDonalds were no exception. In 1777, Jane "Jennie" McCrea, the stepdaughter of Catharine Rosbrugh McCrea McDonald, was murdered in western Vermont, apparently by Indians allied with the British. The brutal act sparked a firestorm of anger that swept through the American colonies and consequently helped to secure an American victory over the British at Saratoga, a critical turning point of the war.[7]

In the midst of it all, the young Richard probably went about his schooling and helped with the farm as needed. He must have received a solid education from his well-to-do McDonald family. Records show his father, Maj. Richard, was involved with the establishment of the Academy of Somerville in 1801.[8] Certainly, the McDonalds were a family that knew the value of education, which had enabled them to rise to prominence in their community. No doubt Maj. Richard hired private tutors, as was the custom in those early days, to properly instruct his children and instill in them knowledge and skills that would help them to succeed in life.

In the winter of 1778-1779, Gen. Henry Knox and his artillery under the overall command of Gen. Washington made their camp in Col. William McDonald's fields at Pluckemin.[9] Col. William was Maj. Richard's father and Richard's grandfather. Known as the Pluckemin Artillery Cantonment, the site is recognized today as the birthplace of the American military training academy, a precursor to West Point. No doubt Col. William and Maj. Richard were instrumental in helping Knox to get situated.

On Feb. 18, 1779, Gen. Knox hosted the Grand Alliance Ball at the Pluckemin Cantonment to celebrate the alliance with France. One of the most extravagant events of the Revolution, the affair included fireworks and an elaborate Greek temple supported by Corinthian columns. Gen. Washington, his wife Martha, Gen. and Mrs. Knox, Gen. Nathanael Greene and many other important dignitaries were in attendance.[10] No doubt the McDonalds were there, too. Young Richard would have been about 17 years old and must have felt very privileged to be a witness to history.

The Revolution would drag on for a few more years. It seems likely that young Richard, like the other men in his family, would have been gripped with patriotic fervor and would have relished the opportunity to take up the musket and join the army. Perhaps he did, but no record has been found to document any service on his part. The family tradition handed down to descendants in his brother William's family says that George Washington himself advised William to stay "at home to take care of the younger children while his father was away in the army." Perhaps Richard was needed at home as well. The McDonalds had mills and other properties, which needed tending.

After the war, in 1786, Samuel McDonald, Col. William's illegitimate son by his mistress Ruth Leferty, scandalized the Somerset County community when he killed John Connet in a fit of rage, presumably in the midst of a dispute with his half-brother, Maj. Richard McDonald.[11] Samuel was tried, found guilty of murder and hanged on Gallows Hill in Somerville.

The event appears to have had a traumatic effect on the entire McDonald family. Thereafter, they must have been subject to a great deal of scorn and derision from the members of their community. There is an indication of this in the surviving records. In subsequent historical accounts, quite a bit of vitriol is directed at Col. William McDonald and his two sons, Bill and Samuel, half-brothers of Maj. Richard. The old Colonel, in a desperate attempt to try to save his son Samuel's life, apparently forged some documents. He had been one of the most powerful men in the county, mind you, High Sheriff of Somerset and a former Justice of the Quorum. His unlawful actions must have seemed particularly egregious in the minds of his fellow citizens.[12]

Despite the difficulties incurred by his father and siblings, Maj. Richard McDonald maintained his dignity and his high status in the community. Nonetheless, most of the McDonalds left the Bedminster area in the years following Samuel's hanging. Maj. Richard's eldest son, William R. McDonald, moved to New York City for a time and in January 1787, married Abigail Fowler in Litchfield County, Connecticut. He went on to Amsterdam, New York, and eventually settled in Herkimer County, New York.

Richard, the second son, may have followed his older brother to New York at least for a short time. Probably about 1787 or 1788,[13] he married Catharine Lansing, the daughter of Levinus and Catherine Lansing, and settled in Lansingburgh, Rensselaer County, New York, about 40 miles southeast of Amsterdam, where his brother was living.

Levinus Lansing Esq.,[14] Richard's father-in-law, was a wealthy landowner whose father, Abraham Jacob Lansing (1720-1791), was the founder of Lansingburgh. The Lansings were originally from Holland, having settled in Albany, New York, as early as 1666.[15]

Levinus Lansing was a Revolutionary War veteran who served in Col. Stephen J. Schuyler's militia in 1777.[16] It is interesting to note that Abraham Ten Eyck was a lieutenant in Col. Schuyler's militia. The Ten Eycks were prominent in the Revolution in Somerset County, New Jersey, as well. Samuel McDonald, the illegitimate son of Col. William McDonald, served in Capt. Jacob Ten Eyck's company of the First Somerset militia.

In 1792, Levinus was President of the Village of Lansingburgh, succeeding his father, Abraham Jacob Lansing, who served in that office in 1791.[17]

Lansingburgh, Rensselaer County, NY
By ZooFari – from official map, CC BY-SA 3.0

Founded about 1770, Lansingburgh is located south of Schaghticoke and north of Troy. The village grew rapidly after 1771 attracting manufacturing and mercantile businesses. A school was founded in 1774. The first church, a Protestant Reformed Dutch Church, which the McDonalds may well have attended, was organized in 1784. A Masonic lodge was instituted in 1787.[18] The First Presbyterian Church was organized in 1792. The walkways leading to the church were made of brick imported from Holland by Levinus Lansing.[19] About 1900, Lansingburgh was annexed by the city of Troy.[20]

Richard McDonald's occupation has not been discovered, but he was probably a landowner, farmer and perhaps a merchant. His son, Richard L., we know, was in the grocery business. The elder Richard and his wife, Catharine, were both pioneers of the area and no doubt had to endure the trials and privations of pioneer life. They had nine known children: six sons and three daughters.

Tragically, both Richard and his wife, Catharine, succumbed to illness within two days of each other. Richard died first, of a fever, on Dec. 20, 1812. Catharine died of a sore throat on Dec. 22, 1812.[21] He was said to be 50 years old. She was 44. They were buried in Oakwood Cemetery, Troy, Rensselaer County, New York.

Forever after, at each Christmas time, their children must have been haunted by grief. Only two of the children were at least 21 years old at the time, Richard L. and his sister, Catharine Adams, the wife of James Adams, Esq.

The other seven children were minors. As orphans, they were probably sent to live with various relatives shortly after the deaths of their parents. As we shall see, little is known of what happened to most of the children.

THE CHILDREN OF RICHARD AND CATHARINE (LANSING) MCDONALD

The will and probate records of Levinus Lansing, Richard's father-in-law, provided much of the documentation for Richard and Catharine (Lansing) McDonald's children.[22] Levinus was baptized Aug. 6, 1749.[23] He wrote his will on Mar. 18, 1829, and died in Lansingburgh on or about Oct. 16, 1836, aged 87.[24]

Richard and Catharine (Lansing) McDonald had six sons and three daughters. Only four of those children are known to have had progeny, and only two, Richard L. McDonald and Elizabeth McDonald Wells, have known living descendants today. There may have been other descendants from the other lines, but they have been lost to history and today have no idea of their McDonald lineage. Perhaps more will be revealed in the future.

Levinus Lansing's will named five of his McDonald grandsons: Richard L., Abraham, Lansing, George and Jacob.[25] This is probably the birth order of the sons of Richard and Catharine (Lansing) McDonald with Richard L. being the oldest and Jacob the youngest.

Little is known of Abraham, the second son, who was no doubt named after his maternal grandfather, Abraham Jacob Lansing, the founder of Lansingburgh. He was born about 1792-1795. In 1820, he was engaged in agriculture in Lansingburgh and living with a female under 16 years of age.[26] The 1836 probate records of Levinus Lansing's estate show Abraham was alive at that time and living in New York. At some point he must have taken a wife. A record of the Rensselaer County Surrogate Court dated 1839 shows he had a son, Benjamin.[27] Whatever happened to Abraham and Benjamin, however, is unknown.

The third son, Lansing, was obviously named in honor of his mother's Lansing family. He was probably born sometime between 1796 and 1802. Lansing was at least 14 years of age on June 20, 1816, when he petitioned the Orphans Court of Somerset County, New Jersey, to appoint his uncle, Col. George McDonald, as his guardian. The documents are signed by Lansing, Col. George McDonald, Samuel Swan (George's brother-in-law), Martin Schenck and Cornelius Van Horn.[28] These documents were the key pieces of evidence that initially linked Col. George McDonald of Somerset County to Lansing McDonald, son of Richard of Rensselaer County, New York. Without them, we wouldn't have been able to definitively tie the Lansingburgh McDonalds to the Somerset County McDonalds. Whatever happened to Lansing is unknown. It appears he was a shoemaker, unmarried and living in Troy, Rensselaer County, in 1850.[29] After that, he disappears from the records.

The fourth son of Richard and Catharine McDonald was not listed among the heirs when his grandfather, Levinus Lansing, wrote his will in 1829. His name was Alanson. He was discovered among Rensselaer County court records, which showed that his elder brother, Richard L. McDonald, was appointed his guardian. The document, dated Jan. 12, 1821, reveals that Alanson was born on Feb. 8, 1802.[30] He probably went to live with brother Richard L. after his parents died in 1812. The fact that Alanson was not named in his grandfather's will suggests that he was deceased by then. He couldn't have been more than 18 years old. The other possibility is that Lansing and Alanson are the same person with one of those names being a middle name.

George, the fifth son of Richard and Catharine, was no doubt named after his uncle George, the lawyer of Somerset County, New Jersey. Like his brother, Alanson, he was placed into the guardianship of his elder brother, Richard L. McDonald. The court papers reveal George was born May 26, 1808.[31] He was only 4 1/2 years old when his parents died. He was alive in 1844 when his aunt Hester Lansing Allen's will was probated. After that, he disappears from the records.

Richard and Catharine's youngest son, Jacob, must have been born between 1809 and 1812. He was just a toddler when his parents died. Levinus Lansing's probate records show he was living in Georgia in 1836.[32] He was still alive in 1844 when his aunt Hester Lansing Allen's will was probated. If he prospered, married and had children, there could be McDonald descendants today living in Georgia and the deep South. Those who wish to know if they are indeed descended from the McDonalds of Somerset County, New Jersey, should join the Clan Donald USA Genetic Genealogy Project and take a Y-DNA test.[33]

The two eldest daughters of Richard and Catharine McDonald, Catharine and Elizabeth, married and had children and will be discussed in subsequent chapters. The youngest daughter, Jane, was probably born between her two brothers, Alanson and George, that is, between 1803 and 1807. She was unmarried in 1829 when her grandfather Levinus wrote his will.[34] Jane died of consumption in September 1834, not more than 31 years old. She died intestate and was buried in Oakwood Cemetery.[35] Her brother, Richard L. McDonald, served as administrator of her estate. The probate records identify her as "Jane McDonald,"[36] yet Oakwood Cemetery records say her surname was Ferrin. Did she, in fact, marry a man named Ferrin? Or was Ferrin perhaps her middle name? We don't know.

Chapter 2

RICHARD L. MCDONALD
(c. 1789 - c. 1869)
and His Descendants

Great Great Grandparents: William and Florance MacDonel
Great Grandparents: Col. William McDonald and Unknown First Wife
Grandparents: Maj. Richard McDonald and Margsrietje Schamp
Parents: Richard McDonald and Catharine Lansing
Siblings: Catharine, Abraham, Lansing, Elizabeth, Alanson, George, Jane, Jacob

RICHARD L. MCDONALD
+ Sophia Van Arnum (c. 1792-1825)

1. Catharine McDonald (c. 1812-aft. 1892, m. Unknown Ransom, Lot Ackley)
2. Levinus McDonald (c. 1816-1892, m. Eliza Barber Patchin, Louisa Unknown)
3. Caroline McDonald (c. 1818-aft. 1850, m. Leonard Ransom)
4. Cornelius McDonald (1820-1849)
5. Henry McDonald (c. 1821-unknown)

+ Susan Rowley (c. 1801-1857)

1. Eldridge McDonald (c. 1831-1834)
2. Charles Richard McDonald (c. 1835-1904, m. Frances H. Drummer, Fannie Dudoire)

According to census records, Richard L. McDonald, the eldest son of Richard and Catharine (Lansing) McDonald, was born about 1789 in Rensselaer County, New York, probably in the vicinity of Lansingburgh.[37] His middle name was probably "Levinus" after his maternal grandfather.

Richard L. married Sophia Van Arnum, the daughter of Levinus and Lydia Van Arnum, about 1811, given the fact that their first child, Catharine, was born about 1812. That same year, in December, Richard L. lost both of his parents unexpectedly to disease within two days of one another. Soon after, he probably had to take on caretaking responsibilities for some of his younger siblings. Indeed, records show he was appointed guardian for his younger brothers, Alanson and George in 1821.[38]

Sophia bore at least four more children: Levinus, Caroline, Cornelius and Henry.[39] The family was living in Lansingburgh in 1820. A free colored female, aged 14-25, was living with them, probably as a servant.[40]

In October 1825, Sophia died in childbirth. She was only 33 years old. She was laid to rest in Oakwood Cemetery, Troy, Rensselaer County, New York.[41]

Richard may have had his hands full for several years raising his young children as a widowed father. He married again on Aug. 12, 1829, to Susan Rowley.[42] She was born about 1802 in Albany County, New York.[43] She was probably the daughter of Eldridge (c. 1779-1849) and Hester (c. 1776-1847) Rowley of Lansingburgh.[44]

Susan and Richard had two children together: Eldridge and Charles Richard.

Eldridge lived only 2 or 3 years, passing on Feb. 15, 1834.[45] Charles, however, had many descendants, some of whom are still living today.

Richard L. McDonald was a grocer by profession, at least by the time the 1850 census was taken.[46] We might wonder if it was a family business handed down by his father, but we simply don't know. We do know that Richard must have been a prominent citizen, well respected in the community. He served as clerk of the village of Lansingburgh in 1836 and 1838 and from 1840-1841. In 1838 and 1839, he was also a Justice of the Peace, following in the footsteps of his grandfather, Col. William McDonald, who also served in that capacity in Somerset County, New Jersey.[47]

Richard's wife, Susan, died on Oct. 23, 1857, at the age of 55. Richard then moved in with his son, Charles, and his wife, Frances. The census of 1860 describes Richard as a gentleman. His real estate was valued at $1200 and his personal estate at $125.[48]

Richard died intestate, probably in early 1869 at the age of 80. His son, Levinus, was named administrator of his estate on Mar. 19, 1869.[49] The burial locations of Richard and his two wives are unknown.

CATHARINE MCDONALD RANSOM ACKLEY (c. 1812-aft. 1892)
(Richard L. McDonald, Richard, Maj. Richard, Col. William, William MacDonel)

Catharine McDonald, the eldest child of Richard L. and Sophia (Van Arnum) McDonald, was born about 1812, probably in Lansingburgh, Rensselaer County, New York.[50] She first married a Mr. Ransom,[51] probably a relation of her sister Caroline's husband, Leonard Ransom. Secondly, she married a stockbroker, Lot Ackley, on July 17, 1855.[52] There are no known children from either of these marriages.

Lot Ackley died sometime between Mar. 21 and May 19, 1865, at the age of 56.[53] Catharine lived quite a bit longer. She was residing in Lansingburgh at the age of 80 in 1892 when her brother Levinus died. She held his funeral service in her home at 838 Third Avenue.[54]

LEVINUS MCDONALD (c. 1816-1892)
(Richard L. McDonald, Richard, Maj. Richard, Col. William, William MacDonel)

Levinus McDonald, the second child of Richard L. and Sophia (Van Arnum) McDonald, was born about 1816, in Rensselaer County, New York.[55] He was no doubt named after his maternal grandfather, Levinus Van Arnum, as well as his paternal great grandfather, Levinus Lansing.

Levinus married Eliza Barber Patchin on Feb. 12, 1840.[56] Both Levinus and Eliza were residents of Troy at the time. They had one child born about 1841, who died July 9, 1842.[57]

Levinus was a draper and tailor, as well as a dealer in foreign and domestic goods. An advertisement for his business in Troy dated Sept. 9, 1942, noted that he had just returned from New York with a selection of cloths, cashmeres, scarfs, handkerchiefs, gloves, suspenders, etc.[58]

We don't know what happened to Levinus's first wife, Eliza Patchin, but by 1855, he had married again to a woman named Louisa. She was born about 1827 in Rensselaer County.[59] They apparently had no issue.

Levinus probably returned to Lansingburgh in his later years. He died there on Apr. 23, 1892, at the age of 76. His funeral was held at his sister Catharine Ackley's house.[60]

CAROLINE MCDONALD RANSOM (c. 1818-aft. 1850) AND FAMILY
(Richard L. McDonald, Richard, Maj. Richard, Col. William, William MacDonel)

Caroline McDonald, the third child of Richard L. and Sophia (Van Arnum) McDonald, was born about 1818, probably in Lansingburgh. On Jan. 7, 1840, when she was about 22 years old, Caroline married Leonard Ransom, who was born about 1816.[61] They had one child, Sidney Smith Ransom, born about 1843.

Leonard Ransom died when he was only 30 years old on Sept. 12, 1846. Caroline and her son, Sidney, were living together in what appears to be a boarding situation in Lansingburgh in 1850.[62] Caroline probably died within the next few years. In 1855, her 12-year-old son, Sidney, was living with his grandfather, Richard L. McDonald.[63]

Leonard and Caroline McDonald Ransom's burial location is unknown.

SIDNEY SMITH RANSOM (c. 1843-aft. 1884) AND FAMILY
(Caroline McDonald Ransom, Richard L. McDonald, Richard, Maj. Richard, Col. William,
   William MacDonel)

Sidney Smith Ransom was the only child of Leonard and Caroline (McDonald) Ransom.[64] His father died when he was only three years old. His mother apparently died by the time he was 12.

He went to live with his grandfather, Richard L. McDonald, for a while, but by 1860, he had moved to Schaghticoke, Rensselaer County, New York, to live with agricultural implement manufacturer Isaac Grant and his family. At the age of 17, Sidney was employed as a clerk and salesman.[65]

In June of 1865, just after the ending of the Civil War, Sidney was living in Hoosick, Rensselaer County, as a boarder in the house of Annis Burtis.[66] By 1870, he had moved to Monroe, Colusa County, California, to take up residence with the merchant Samuel J. Davis and his family. Sidney was working as a saloonkeeper with a personal estate valued at $2000, a portion of which may have been inherited from his parents.[67]

Probably about 1871, Sidney married Mary H. Calden. She was born in Maine about 1849. They had a daughter, Caloise, born about 1872.

By 1880, the family was living in Oakland, Alameda County, California, with Sidney's in-laws, Alburn and Mary Calden. Sidney was working in a livery stable at the time.[68] A second child, Irma W., was born about 1882.

In 1884, when he was about 41 years old, Sidney was again working as a saloonkeeper. This time in South Red Bluff, Tehama County, California.[69] Sometime after 1884 he died. Where and when is a mystery.

In any case, his widow, Mary H. Calden Ransom, was living in San Francisco in 1900.[70] She and her two daughters were living in the household of Mary's son-in-law Guy Calden, the husband of daughter Caloise. They had moved to Oakland by 1910.[71]

In 1911, the U. S. City Directory shows Mary H. Calden Ransom was still living in Oakland. She was about 62 years old.[72] That is the last we hear of her.

CALOISE RANSOM CALDEN (1872-1910) AND FAMILY
(Sidney S. Ransom, Caroline McDonald Ransom, Richard L. McDonald, Richard, Maj. Richard,
  Col. William, William MacDonel)

Caloise Ransom, the first of two daughters of Sidney Smith and Mary H. (Calden) Ransom, was born about 1872 in California.[73] About 1892, she married Guy Chester Calden, a letter carrier with dark blue eyes and blonde hair, who was born in California on Jan. 21, 1871.[74] The son of Frederick R. and Helena (Browne) Calden, Guy appears to be distantly related to Caloise's branch of the Calden family.[75] In fact, before Guy and Caloise were born, Guy's parents were living with Caloise's mother and grandparents in 1870 in Monroe, Colusa County, California.[76]

Guy and Caloise (Ransom) Calden had two children:
1. Ruth Ransom (1893-1983, m. Reed Walgamott Robinson)
2. Guy Cecil (1895-1967, m. Margaret Elizabeth Leach)

From 1894-1896, Guy served as a lieutenant (junior grade) in the 1st Division Naval Battalion of the National Guard of California, headquartered in San Francisco.[77] By 1900, he was an attorney living with his family in San Francisco.[78] Also in his household at that time were his mother-in-law, Mary H. Calden Ransom, and sister-in-law, Irma W. Ransom, who married Arthur Edward Ladewig about two years later and moved to Oakland.[79]

The Caldens must have been witness to, and survived, the great San Francisco Earthquake of April 18, 1906, one of the worst natural disasters in U.S. history. By 1910, they had all moved to Oakland. Guy had established his own law practice at that time. [80]

That same year, on Aug. 16, Caloise died after a long illness. She was only 37 years old. Her obituary said she "was a prominent club worker of this city and deeply loved by a wide circle of friends."[81]

Guy was much more fortunate in that he lived a very long life. He died in Alameda County on Mar. 5, 1960, at the age of 89.[82]

RUTH RANSOM CALDEN ROBINSON (1893-1983) AND FAMILY
(Caloise Ransom Calden, Sidney S. Ransom, Caroline McDonald Ransom, Richard L. McDonald, Richard, Maj. Richard, Col. William, William MacDonel)

Ruth Ransom Calden, the eldest of two children of Guy Sr. and Caloise (Ransom) Calden, was born in California on Apr. 8, 1893.[83] She went to the University of California at Berkeley, became a member of the Alpha Xi Delta Sorority and Sigma Kappa Alpha, the history honor society, and graduated in 1918.[84]

On Mar. 5, 1921, in Alameda County, California,[85] she married Reed Walgamott Robinson, a veteran of World War I.[86] The son of John and Ida (Walgamott) Robinson, Reed was tall and slender with gray eyes and brown hair.[87] He was born Aug. 5, 1891, in Croley near Clinton, Hickman County, Kentucky.[88]

Reed was a successful businessman, a general partner in Golden Nugget Sweets, Ltd., a candy bar manufacturer whose headquarters was located at 1975 Market St. in San Francisco across from the U.S. Mint. In 1955, Reed was elected president of the Redwood Empire Association.[89]

Reed and Ruth (Calden) Robinson had two children:
1. Caloise Ransom (1923-1999, m. John Merritt Tucker)
2. Nancy Ida (b. Feb 21, 1927, attended University of California, Berkeley)[90]

Reed passed away on June 12, 1970, in San Francisco. He was 78 years old.[91] Ruth lived to be 90. She died on Dec. 26, 1983.

CALOISE RANSOM ROBINSON TUCKER (1923-1999) AND FAMILY
(Ruth Calden Robinson, Caloise Ransom Calden, Sidney S. Ransom, Caroline McDonald Ransom, Richard L. McDonald, Richard, Maj. Richard, Col. William, William MacDonel)

Caloise Ransom Robinson, the eldest child of Reed and Ruth (Calden) Robinson, was born Dec. 11, 1923, in Oakland, Alameda County, California.[92] Named after her maternal grandmother, Caloise Ransom Calden, she attended the University of California, Berkeley.[93]

Caloise married John Merritt "Jack" Tucker, the son of Clarence R. and Alice E. (Merritt) Tucker. Jack was born on Jan. 26, 1920, in Baltimore, Maryland.[94] He was a USMC veteran of World War II. After the war, he joined the Chubb Group of Insurance Companies. In 1967, he and his family moved to Atlanta, Georgia, where he became manager of Chubb's southeast operations. Bill Pritchard, a colleague of his, said that Jack was "the finest quality of businessman... a delightful companion, always genial and easy-going."[95]

When he retired, Jack remained very active in his community. He served as a mediator for 15 years. Edith Primm, senior adviser of the Justice Center of Atlanta, said, "He handled all manner of conflicts at our center, from neighborhood quarrels to business disputes... He treated the people who come to us in a kind and respectful way and guided them to agreeable compromises to disputes that seemed insoluble. He was equally conscientious serving for 10 years with a panel that advised Fulton County Juvenile Court judges concerning questions of custody of abused and abandoned children."[96]

Jack and Caloise loved to travel and see the world. They visited every continent and at least 80 countries. Jack was an enthusiastic photographer, but he suffered from macular degeneration, which obstructed his field of vision. When he returned from his trips, he would have his photos blown up several sizes and then exclaim, "So that's what I saw!"[97]

Diminished eyesight didn't stop him from playing golf, either. "We played golf regularly the last 10 years, and although Jack could barely see, he always beat me," remembered Ken Black, retired dean of Georgia State University Business School. "Even when I was a stroke or so up on him going to the 18th hole, he'd find a way to come out on top."[98]

Jack's wife, Caloise Robinson Tucker, passed away on Sept. 3, 1999, at the age of 75.[99] Jack went to live at Lenbrook Square, a retirement community. He continued to be a positive force in many people's lives.

Debbie Taylor, president of Lenbrook Square marveled at Jack's ability to get around even with his visual difficulties, "For others like him here, he taught classes in coping strategies or counseled them one-on-one. He kept up with all the new technical aids for the partially sighted, but more importantly, he projected a positive attitude. He was one of the kindest, most compassionate people I've known."[100]

Clare Alexander, a resident of Lenbrook Square, was very appreciative of Jack's help and expertise. "Anytime you needed a visual aid, Jack would order it on his computer, then instruct you on how to use it," she said. "He helped me get a recording device with buttons large enough. I use it to play talking books."[101]

Jack died of congestive heart failure on June 17, 2004, at the age of 84.[102] His memorial was held at Episcopal Cathedral of Saint Philip in Atlanta.[103]

Jack and Caloise are survived by their children, Guy Tucker and Carol Tucker Graham, and three grandchildren.[104]

GUY CECIL CALDEN (1895-1967)
(Caloise Ransom Calden, Sidney S. Ransom, Caroline McDonald Ransom, Richard L. McDonald, Richard, Maj. Richard, Col. William, William MacDonel)

Guy Cecil Calden,[105] the second child of Guy Chester and Caloise (Ransom) Calden, was born Dec. 13, 1895, in San Francisco, California. He completed four years of high school. A veteran of World War I, on May 12, 1917, at about age 22, he sailed to France to serve in the American Ambulance Corps.[106]

When he was 30 years old, on Aug. 7, 1926, Guy married Margaret Elizabeth Leach, the daughter of Frank A. and Margaret Leach. Margaret was born Mar. 21, 1896, in California, and had completed two years of college.[107]

Guy was employed as a special agent of the Standard Oil Company. He and Margaret were living in South Pasadena, Los Angeles County, California, in 1930, and had moved to Fresno, Fresno County, California, by 1940.[108] They had no children.

Margaret Leach Calden died on Dec. 9, 1960, in Santa Barbara County, California, at the age of 64.

On Dec. 16, 1961, Guy married Gertrude L. Beckwith Macmillan in Santa Barbara County, California. She was born Apr. 18, 1909, in Ventura County, California.[109] Guy died a few years later on Aug. 7, 1967, at the age of 71.[110]

Gertrude lived quite a bit longer. She died at the age of 92 on July 1, 2001, and was buried in Santa Barbara Cemetery in Santa Barbara.[111]

IRMA W. RANSOM LADEWIG (c. 1882-1934) AND FAMILY
(Sidney S. Ransom, Caroline McDonald Ransom, Richard L. McDonald, Richard, Maj. Richard, Col. William, William MacDonel)

Irma W. Ransom, the second child of Sidney S. and Mary H. (Calden) Ransom, was born about 1882 in California.[112] About 1902, she married Arthur Edward Ladewig, the son of Henry Francis and Helen (Garner) Ladewig.[113] A real estate broker, Arthur was born in Queensland, Australia, on Feb. 22, in 1876 or 1877.[114] Tall and stout, he was a bald-headed fellow with blue eyes.

Arthur and Irma (Ransom) Ladewig had four children:
1. Virginia Mary (1902-1978, m. Cecil Jerome Hawkins)
2. George Willard (1904-1985, m. Leota Dulcie Smith)
3. Edward Garner (1905-1974, m. Eleanor Van Stone)
4. John Ransom (1907-1983, m. Bernice Florence Roth)

Irma passed away in San Francisco at 51 years old on Apr. 22, 1934. Arthur died on Jan. 22, 1945, in Siskiyou Co., California. He was 68.[115]

VIRGINIA MARY LADEWIG HAWKINS (1902-1978) AND FAMILY
(Irma Ransom Ladewig, Sidney S. Ransom, Caroline McDonald Ransom, Richard L. McDonald, Richard,
  Maj. Richard, Col. William, William MacDonel)

Virginia Mary Ladewig, the eldest child of Arthur Edward and Irma W. (Ransom) Ladewig, was born Nov. 18, 1902, in California.[116] She graduated from high school and on May 15, 1923, in Alameda County, California, married Cecil Jerome Hawkins, the son of Alfred N. and Emma (Sherman) Hawkins.[117] Cecil was a high school graduate as well. He was born in Woodland, Yolo County, California, on Oct. 4, 1896.[118]

Virginia and Cecil had one daughter, Geraldine, born about 1928. The family was living in Berkeley, Alameda County, California, in 1940. An auditor by profession, Cecil was working in San Francisco for the State of California Board of Equalization, which was involved with administering California's sales and use, fuel, alcohol, tobacco and other taxes.[119]

Virginia died in Alameda County on Jan. 19, 1978, at the age of 75. Her husband, Cecil, passed away on July 28, 1991, in Riverside County, California. He was 94.[120]

GEORGE WILLARD LADEWIG (1904-1985) AND FAMILY
(Irma Ransom Ladewig, Sidney S. Ransom, Caroline McDonald Ransom, Richard L. McDonald, Richard,
  Maj. Richard, Col. William, William MacDonel)

George Willard Ladewig, the second child of Arthur Edward and Irma W. (Ransom) Ladewig, was born May 27, 1904, in California.[121] He was highly educated, having completed 5 years of college.[122] In 1930, he was living with his brother John and his family in Nevada, Merced County, California. He was engaged in cotton farming.

George married Leota Dulcie Smith, the daughter of Joel Pruitt and Ruth A. (Isaacs) Smith.[123] Leota was born June 13, 1898, in California.[124] They were living in Oakland, Alameda County, by 1940, at which time George was a farm implement salesman.

Both George and Leota died at the age of 81. Leota went first on May 25, 1980, in Siskiyou County, California. George followed on Aug. 24, 1985, in Modoc, Siskiyou County.[125]

George and Leota (Smith) Ladewig had a son, Richard Edward Ladewig.

RICHARD EDWARD LADEWIG (1936-Living) AND FAMILY
(George W. Ladewig, Irma Ransom Ladewig, Sidney S. Ransom, Caroline McDonald Ransom, Richard L.
  McDonald, Richard, Maj. Richard, Col. William, William MacDonel)

Richard Edward Ladewig, the son of George Willard and Leota (Smith) Ladewig, was born Oct. 25, 1936, in Alameda County, California.[126] He married Donna June Cashe, the daughter of Don and Nora Ann (Querry) Cash, on Oct. 25, 1954, in Siskiyou County. Donna was born Dec. 14, 1937. [127]

Richard and Donna (Cash) Ladewig have four children:
  1. Pamela Kay (b. 1955)

2. Michael Edward (b. 1957)
3. Lynn Marie (b. 1958)
4. John Edward (b. 1964)[128]

EDWARD GARNER LADEWIG (1905-1974) AND FAMILY
(Irma Ransom Ladewig, Sidney S. Ransom, Caroline McDonald Ransom, Richard L. McDonald, Richard,
 Maj. Richard, Col. William, William MacDonel)

Edward Garner Ladewig, the third child of Arthur Edward and Irma W. (Ransom) Ladewig, was born June 27, 1905, in Oakland, Alameda County, California.[129]

Edward received a college education and launched his career as a purser (head steward) on the Dollar Steamship Lines in 1925 in San Francisco. Two years later, he was an employee of the Tropical Oil Company in Boston, Massachusetts. In 1934, he was appointed assistant export manager for the Gillette company, also in Boston.[130]

About 1935, Edward married Eleanor Van Stone, the daughter of Edward Paul and Anna Gertrude Van Stone.[131] Eleanor was a college graduate born in Massachusetts on Aug. 21, 1911.[132]

In 1944, Edward began to work for Bristol-Myers, the pharmaceutical company. He was eventually promoted to president of Britol-Myers International Division, in which capacity he served until he retired. He was also a director of the Far East-American Council and a member of the National Foreign Trade Council.[133]

Edward died on Feb. 27, 1974, in Fairfield County, Connecticut, at the age of 68. His wife, Eleanor, passed on Jan. 26, 1993, in Fairfield, Fairfield County, aged 81.[134]

Edward Garner and Eleanor (Van Stone) Ladewig had two children:
1. David Edward (b. 1941, m. Stephanie Illes)
2. Margot Van Stone (m. David N. Miles)[135]

JOHN RANSOM LADEWIG (1907-1983) AND FAMILY
(Irma Ransom Ladewig, Sidney S. Ransom, Caroline McDonald Ransom, Richard L. McDonald, Richard,
 Maj. Richard, Col. William, William MacDonel)

John Ransom Ladewig, the fourth and youngest child of Arthur Edward and Irma W. (Ransom) Ladewig, was born Sept. 7, 1907, in California.[136] He graduated from high school and married Bernice Florence Roth. She was born May 28, 1907, in California.[137]

John was a farmer.

Bernice Roth Ladewig died on Nov. 8, 1982, in Humboldt County, California, at age 75. John died a few months later on Jan. 29, 1983, also aged 75.[138] They were buried in Sunrise Cemetery, Fortuna, Humboldt County, California.[139]

They had one daughter, Barbara Jean Ladewig, born Mar. 6, 1926, in Alameda County, California. She married a Mr. Simpson and died on Apr. 7, 1987, in Humboldt County, California, aged 61.[140]

———⊂━≣⊃———

CORNELIUS MCDONALD (c. 1820-1849)
(Richard L. McDonald, Richard, Maj. Richard, Col. William, William MacDonel)

Cornelius McDonald, the fourth child of Richard L. and Sophia (Van Arnum) McDonald, was born about 1820, probably in Lansingburgh, Rensselaer County, New York. He was named as an heir of his grandfather, Levinus Van Arnum, but he died on June 7, 1849, at the age of about 29, before the probate was completed.[141] His share of the inheritance was assigned to his brother, Levinus. It is not known whether or not Cornelius married and had children.

HENRY MCDONALD (c. 1821-unknown)
(Richard L. McDonald, Richard, Maj. Richard, Col. William, William MacDonel)

Henry McDonald, the fifth child of Richard L. and Sophia (Van Arnum) McDonald, was probably born between 1821 and 1825, that is between the birth of his elder brother Cornelius and the death of his mother, Sophia, in Oct. 1825. He was entitled to an inheritance from his grandfather, Levinus Van Arnum, but his share was assigned to his brother, Levinus, suggesting that he may have been deceased before the probate was completed in 1850.[142]

CHARLES RICHARD MACDONALD (c. 1835-1904) AND FAMILY
(Richard L. McDonald, Richard, Maj. Richard, Col. William, William MacDonel)

Charles Richard MacDonald, the second child of Richard L. McDonald by his second wife, Susan Rowley, was born about Apr. 1835, in Rensselaer County, New York.[143] Apparently, he changed the spelling of the family name to MacDonald, a spelling carried on by his descendants.

Charles was a clerk living with his parents in Lansingburgh in 1850. He may have been working in his father's grocery business at that time. Later census records show Charles became a brush maker in a brush factory.

On Jan. 2, 1860, when he was about 25 years old, he married Frances H. "Fanny" Drummer.[144] They had six children:
1. Ida (c. 1860- aft.1880)
2. Fanny (c. 1867-aft 1880)
3. George D. (1867-1872)[145]
4. Bertha (c. 1870-aft. 1880)
5. Angie B. (c. 1872-1873)[146]
6. Frank (c. 1875-aft. 1880)

Unfortunately, we know very little of what happened to the children. Two of them, George and Angie, died very young.

In 1880, the family was living in Lansingburgh. The eldest daughter, Ida, was clerking in a store. After that date, she disappears from the records, along with her sisters Fanny and Bertha and her brother Frank. They may have married and had children, but no evidence has yet been found.

Charles's first wife, Frances Drummer MacDonald, must have died sometime before 1891.

On Jan. 24, 1891, in Green Island, Albany County, New York, Charles took a second wife, Fannie Dudoire, a French Canadian immigrant born about 1869. Rev. E. A. Eaton presided over the ceremony.[147] Both Charles and Fannie were living in Troy at the time.

Charles and Fannie (Dudoire) MacDonald had a son, Richard Earl MacDonald, born in Lansingburgh on Sept. 13, 1894.[148]

Charles died on Oct. 1, 1904, in Troy, Rensselaer County, New York, at the age of 69.[149] In 1910, his widow, Fannie, and their son, Richard Earl, were living on their own in Albany. She was working as a button-holer in a shirt factory to make ends meet.

By 1920, Fannie had married again to Thomas Bayliss (or Baylies), who was born about 1870 in England. He was employed as a stationary engineer for a laundry business. They were living in Albany as late as 1930, both about 60 years old. Fannie passed away about 1946, when she was about 76 years old.[150]

RICHARD EARL MACDONALD SR. (1894-1980) AND FAMILY
(Charles R. MacDonald, Richard L., Richard, Maj. Richard, Col. William, William MacDonel)

Richard Earl MacDonald, the only known child of Charles R. MacDonald by his second wife, Fannie Dudoire, was born on Sept. 13, 1894, in Lansingburgh, Rensselaer County, New York.[151] He attended school through the 8th grade.

In 1917, when he registered for the draft in World War I, he was of medium height and build with brown eyes and black hair. He was single, living in Albany and working as a brakeman for the railroad.[152] He signed his name "MacDonald" on his registration.

Richard served as a flight sergeant in the 248th Aero Squadron of the American Expeditionary Forces in World War I.[153] The squadron was involved in training in England from March 18, 1918, to March 1919.[154]

Sometime between 1917 and 1920, Richard married Margaret Mary Schafer, the daughter of Joseph T. and Anna M. (Segar) Schafer.[155] Margaret was born June 16, 1894.[156] She had completed three years of high school.

In 1920, Richard was a bondsman for the railroad in Albany, and by1930, he was a conductor for a steam railroad in Bethlehem, Albany County, New York.[157]

Richard Earl and Margaret (Schafer) MacDonald had four children:
1. Richard Earl Jr. (1920-1997, m. Patricia A. Klein)
2. Joan Marie (1922-1998, m. Frank Joseph Stapf Sr.)
3. Raymond Charles (1924-2011, m. Ann Marie Burry)
4. Jeanne Frances (1926-Living, m. Caley E. Augustine)

Richard died on March 13, 1980, in Albany, at the age of 85.[158] His wife, Margaret, predeceased him on Aug. 15, 1967, aged 73.[159]

RICHARD EARL MACDONALD JR. (1920-1997) AND FAMILY
(Richard E. MacDonald Sr., Charles R., Richard L., Richard, Maj. Richard, Col. William, William MacDonel)

Richard Earl MacDonald Jr., the eldest child of Richard Earl and Margaret (Schafer) MacDonald, was born on Aug. 8, 1920, in Albany, Albany County, New York.[160] In 1940, he was working as a messenger for a steam railroad in Bethlehem, Albany County, New York.

Richard served in the U.S. Navy during World War II as a fire control man first class (FC1).[161]

Richard married Patricia Ann Klein, who was born Dec. 27, 1918.[162] They had one known son, Michael Anthony, born 1948.

Patricia Klein MacDonald died on July 27, 1992, in Citrus County, Florida.[163] She was 73. Her husband, Richard, died on Dec. 4, 1997, in Orange County, Florida. He was 77.[164] They were buried in Our Lady Help of Christians Cemetery, Glenmont, Albany County, New York.[165]

MICHAEL ANTHONY MACDONALD (1948-2008)
(Richard E. MacDonald Jr., Richard E. Sr., Charles R., Richard L., Richard, Maj. Richard, Col. William, William MacDonel)

Michael Anthony "Mike" MacDonald, the son of Richard Earl Jr. and Patricia Ann (Klein) MacDonald, was born on Aug. 19, 1948.[166] He was a P.F.C. in the U.S. Army in the Vietnam War. A resident of Homosassa Springs, Citrus County, Florida, he died in May 2008, aged 59. He is buried in Our Lady Help of Christians Cemetery, Glenmont, Albany County, New York.[167]

JOAN MARIE MACDONALD STAPF (1922-1998) AND FAMILY
(Richard E. MacDonald Sr., Charles R., Richard L., Richard, Maj. Richard, Col. William, William MacDonel)

Joan Marie MacDonald, the second child of Richard Earl and Margaret (Schafer) MacDonald, was born on Oct. 16, 1922, in Albany, Albany County, New York.[168] She attended Bethlehem Central High School in Bethlehem, Albany County, and married Frank Joseph Stapf Sr. on Jan. 26, 1946.[169] He was born Jan. 18, 1922, in Albany, the son of Joseph Frank and Edith (Krouse) Stapf.[170]

Frank Stapf was a U.S. Navy veteran of World War II having served on the USS *Wilson* (DD-408), a Benham-class destroyer.[171] He enlisted on June 26, 1942, and was released just after Christmas on Dec. 28, 1945.[172]

The *Wilson* saw quite a bit of action during the war. In 1943, the ship joined in the fighting off Guadalcanal and participated in the landings on the Japanese-held Russell Islands. In the summer of 1944, the ship was assigned with carrier task forces involved in the Marianas Campaign and the Battle of the Philippine Sea. On Jan. 25, 1944, the *Wilson* was attached to a force that included the carrier USS *Bunker Hill* (CV-17) and the battleships *Iowa* (BB-61) and *New Jersey* (BB-62). They participated in strikes against Kwajalein Atoll in the Marshall Islands.[173]

One of *Wilson's* most harrowing experiences occurred on Apr. 16, 1945, off Kerama Retto near Okinawa, when she was hit by a kamikaze.[174] The gunners opened up a punishing fire on two approaching Japanese planes. They took out the lead plane and knocked down the second sending it crashing into the water about 75 yards off the ship's starboard quarter, but the enemy was not yet finished.

> The plane bounced off the water and came toward Wilson, the propeller striking and lodging into the 40-millimeter gun tub. The plane itself then spun around and passed between 5-inch guns number 3 and 4, and splashed into the sea on the port side, taking with it "a few incidentals such as mooring reels and loose gear." A 250 kilogram bomb carried by the plane passed through the skin of the ship just above the waterline on the starboard side and finally came to rest in an after living compartment. Only the booster charge exploded causing some internal damage to the ship: shrapnel penetrated into adjacent fuel tanks, rupturing the tank bulkheads and the main lead to group three magazines, resulting in minor fires and the flooding of those magazines. Tragically, five men, whose station was in the group three magazine, were killed by drowning and burns as a result of the rupture of the sprinkling system. Three other men were blown overboard at the time the plane hit, and two of them received serious injuries. Fortunately, the ship had been in a turn when she was hit; so she continued on around and managed to pick up her men after completing the circle, bringing them on board for medical treatment.[175]

After the war, Frank Stapf worked as an insurance salesman for several years for the Maryland Casualty Co.,[176] then joined Spancrete Northeast in South Bethlehem, also as a salesman. When he retired in 1981, he was a vice president of that company.

Frank and Joan lived in Colonie, Albany County, New York, for many years, before moving to Port Charlotte, Charlotte County, Florida, in 1983. They attended St. Clare's Catholic Church in Colonie. Frank was a member of the Elks, the American Legion and was past master of the Mt. Vernon Masonic Lodge in Albany.[177]

Joan died on Dec. 5, 1998, in Charlotte County, Florida, at the age of 76.[178] Frank died on Apr. 3, 2009, in Schenectady, Schenectady County, New York, aged 87.[179]

Frank and Joan Marie (MacDonald) Stapf had four children: Robert, Dennis, Deborah, and Frank Jr. [180]

RAYMOND CHARLES MACDONALD (1924-2011)
(Richard E. MacDonald Sr., Charles R., Richard L., Richard, Maj. Richard, Col. William, William MacDonel)

Raymond Charles MacDonald, the third child of Richard Earl and Margaret (Schafer) MacDonald, was born on Mar. 13, 1924, in Albany, Albany County, New York.[181] He graduated from Bethlehem Central High School.

Raymond joined the U.S. Navy in World War II and served as a radioman aboard the USS *LSM-216,* a landing ship.[182] He participated in the assault on Iwo Jima in February 1945. In fact, his ship can be seen in action off Yellow Beach, Iwo Jima, on Feb. 19, 1945, in the film *To the Shores of Iwo Jima,* produced by the U.S. Marine Corps in 1945.[183]

On July 26, 1947, Raymond married Ann Marie Burry, the daughter of Alfred Arthur and Jane Mary (Farren) Burry, in St. James Catholic Church in Albany, Albany County, New York, with Rev. Joseph A. Dunning, officiating.[184]

> The bride wore a white gown with lace bodice and satin skirt and train. She carried a prayer book with a white orchid and a shower of roses.[185]

Ann was born in Albany on Aug. 4, 1923.[186] She was a graduate of the College of Saint Rose in Albany. Her mother, Jane Farren Burry, was born in Ireland.

Raymond was an employee of Otis Elevator Company in Albany, and past president of the International Union of Elevator Constructors Local 35. Otis manufactured elevators, escalators and moving walkways.

In 1982, Raymond and Ann moved to Port Charlotte, Charlotte County, Florida. Raymond was very active in the community as a member of the St. Vincent De Paul Society, The Elks Lodge, the Knights of Columbus Council 5399, and the Charlotte County Antique Car Collectors Club. He was also a communicant and Eucharistic minister at St. Charles Borromeo Catholic Church in Port Charlotte. Politically, he was a Democrat.[187]

Ann Burry MacDonald died on May 10, 2000, aged 76. Raymond passed away on Oct. 18, 2011, at the Baystate Medical Center in Springfield, Hampden County, Massachusetts.[188] Both were buried in Boca Raton Municipal Cemetery and Mausoleum, Boca Raton, Palm Beach County, Florida.[189]

Raymond and Ann (Burry) MacDonald had three children:
1. Jane (m. Roger Lang; children: Elizabeth, Katherine)
2. Joanne (m. Peter Miller; children: Peter, Gregory, Jeffery, Lauren)
3. Raymond Jr. (m. Unknown; children: Raymond III, Ryan)[190]

Raymond MacDonald Jr. and his sons, Raymond III and Ryan, are the only known living male descendants of Richard and Catharine (Lansing) McDonald who still bear the MacDonald surname. It is hoped that one of them will take a Y-DNA test in order to conclusively establish their descent from the McDonalds of Somerset County, New Jersey.[191]

JEANNE FRANCES MACDONALD AUGUSTINE (1924-2016) AND FAMILY
(Richard E. MacDonald Sr., Charles R., Richard L., Richard, Maj. Richard, Col. William, William MacDonel)

Jeanne Frances MacDonald, the fourth child of Richard Earl and Margaret (Schafer) MacDonald, was born on Sept. 15, 1926, in New York.[192] She married Caley Edmond Augustine, the son of Joseph and Josephine (Scannella) Augustine. He was born Mar. 9, 1918, in Clearfield County, Pennsylvania.[193] In 1940, he was working as a line keeper for the railroad and living in Bethlehem, Albany County, New York.[194]

Caley was a U.S. Army veteran of World War II, having served as 1st sergeant of Company I of the 28th Infantry Regiment, 8th Infantry Division.[195] The 28th Infantry landed on Utah Beach as part of the Normandy Invasion on July 4, 1944. It established a bridgehead over the Ay River, which allowed armored divisions to carry out operations in Brittany and Northern France. During ten months of combat, the regiment captured over 115,000 prisoners.[196]

Jeanne was a homemaker and of the Roman Catholic faith. She and Caley had five children: Margaret, Caley, Joseph, Matthew and Patricia.

Caley died on July 7, 2000, aged 82.[197] His wife Jeanne passed away January 8, 2016, aged 89. Both are buried in Royal Palm Memorial Gardens, Punta Gorda, Charlotte County, Florida.[198]

Chapter 3

CATHARINE MCDONALD ADAMS
(c. 1790 - aft. 1818)
and Her Descendants

Great Great Grandparents: William and Florance MacDonel
Great Grandparents: Col. William McDonald and Unknown First Wife
Grandparents: Maj. Richard McDonald and Margrietje Schamp
Parents: Richard McDonald and Catharine Lansing
Siblings: Richard L., Abraham, Lansing, Elizabeth, Alanson, George, Jane, Jacob

CATHARINE MCDONALD (c. 1790 - aft. 1818)
+ James Adams (c. 1780 -1818)
1. Ann Alida Adams (c. 1807-1840, m. Anson H. DeLamater)
2. George Washington Adams (c. 1811-1884, m. Lydia H. Fowler)
3. Catherine Lansing Adams (c. 1812-aft. 1818)
4. James Elisha Adams (c. 1813-aft. 1836)
5. Elizabeth Adams (c. 1814-aft. 1836)

Catharine McDonald, the second child and eldest daughter of Richard and Catharine (Lansing) McDonald, was born about 1790-1791, probably in Lansingburgh, Rensselaer County, New York.[199] She was no doubt named after her mother, Catharine Lansing McDonald.

On June 24, 1808, at the Reformed Dutch Church of the Boght in Albany, Albany County, New York, Catharine married James Adams Esq.,[200] the son of Elisha and Alida (Vanderheyden) Adams.[201] Also known as Jacobus, James was baptized at the Schagticoke Dutch Reformed Church on June 4, 1780.[202]

On July 1, 1818, James Adams signed his Last Will and Testament. He died sometime before Aug. 3, 1818, when the will was probated in Rensselaer County.[203] In the will, James lists his five children, presumably in order of their birth: Ann Alida, George Washington, Catherine Lansing, James Elisha and Elizabeth.

James was only about 38 years old when he died. His wife, Catharine, probably did not live long either. She was not mentioned in her grandfather Levinus Lansing's will in 1829. She must have been deceased by then.

Of their children, very little is known of three of them: Catherine Lansing, James Elisha and Elizabeth. Catherine Lansing Adams disappears from the records after being mentioned in her father's will. James Elisha and Elizabeth Adams were mentioned as heirs in an 1836 probate record for Levinus Lansing in which Henry Bristol was named as their guardian.[204] How the rest of their lives transpired is a mystery.

Sadly, there are no known living descendants of James and Catharine (McDonald) Adams.

ANN ALIDA ADAMS DELAMATER (C. 1807-1840)
(Catharine McDonald Adams, Richard McDonald, Maj. Richard, Col. William, William MacDonel)

Ann Alida Adams, the eldest child of James and Catharine (McDonald) Adams, was no doubt named in part in honor of her paternal grandmother, Alida Vanderheyden. Her gravestone indicates she was born about 1807.[205] If true, Ann Alida must have been born out of wedlock, her parents having married in June of 1808. It seems more likely the gravestone is in error. It seems to be a replacement of an earlier stone for her. She was probably born in 1809, a good nine months after the marriage of her parents.

In 1831, in Madison County, New York, Ann Alida married Anson H. DeLamater, the son of John and Zoa (Eaton) DeLamater.[206] Anson was born on Apr. 13, 1811, in Pompey, Onondaga County, New York.[207] He attended Cazenovia Seminary established by the Methodist Episcopal Church in Cazenovia, New York. Possessed of an adventurous spirit, young Anson headed west in 1834 to seek his fortune in the wilderness of the Michigan frontier. After staking his claim near Clark's Lake, he was elected the first surveyor of Jackson County, Michigan, in 1837, and held that position for 12 straight years. As historian Charles V. DeLand said of him, "Probably there is not another family in Jackson County that has been more closely identified with the early history, growth and development of this, one of the most prolific counties in the Peninsular state, than Anson H. DeLamater and his brothers. Having come to Jackson county at a time when the prairies and forests were in their primeval state, he had an experience that justly earned him the venerable title of pioneer."[208]

Following their marriage, Ann Alida lived for only another nine years. She died on Oct. 14, 1840, not more than 33 years of age.[209] She did not have children.

Anson married twice more: first to Lydia Ann Parmater in 1842, then to Hannah Waite Pierce in 1848.[210]

In 1842, Anson was chosen to represent his district in the Michigan state legistlature. In 1880 and again in 1881, he was elected president of the Pioneer Society of Jackson County.

> In personal appearance Mr. DeLamater was a little above the medium height, and stood erect. His genial countenance bespoke the force of character and the warm and passionate heart that made him a friend to the friendless, a father to the fatherless, and a ready helper to the poor and needy... one of the best remembered of our pioneer citizens.[211]

Anson passed away on his farm on Feb. 22, 1898, at the age of 86. He and Ann Alida now rest in East Liberty Cemetery, Liberty, Jackson County, Michigan.[212]

GEORGE WASHINGTON ADAMS (1811-1884) AND FAMILY
(Catharine McDonald Adams, Richard McDonald, Maj. Richard, Col. William, William MacDonel)

George Washington Adams, the second child of James and Catharine (McDonald) Adams, was born Jan. 12, 1811, in Lansingburgh, Rensselaer County, New York.[213]

On Jan. 21, 1836, he married Lydia H. Fowler, the daughter of James and Jane Fowler, in the State Street Methodist Episcopal Church in Troy, Rensselaer County, New York.[214] Lydia was born Sept. 21, 1817, in Brunswick, Rensselaer County, New York.[215] It is interesting to note that William R. McDonald, son of Maj. Richard McDonald of Somerset County, New Jersey, married Abigail Fowler in Litchfield County, Connecticut, in 1787. Perhaps the Fowlers were a family well known to the McDonalds.

George and Lydia (Fowler) Adams had five children:
1. Elizabeth (c. 1838-aft 1855)
2. Sarah (c. 1838-aft 1855)
3. Cornelius (1843-1847)
4. Emma (c. 1847-1870, m. Unknown Geer)
5. Ellen "Addie" (c. 1854-aft. 1930, m. George A. Main)

In 1855, George W. Adams and his family were living in Brunswick, Rensselaer County, New York. He was working as a laborer.[216] In 1880, when he was about 69, George and Lydia were living with their daughter, Ellen "Addie" and her husband, George Main, in Troy.

George W. Adams died on June 22, 1884, aged 73.[217] His wife, Lydia, passed on May 21, 1889, aged 71.[218] Both were buried in Oakwood Cemetery in Troy.

George and Lydia's two eldest daughters, Elizabeth and Sarah, were apparently twins. They disappear after the 1855 New York State census. Cornelius Adams died of croup on Nov. 10, 1847, at the age of 4 years and 10 days. He was buried in Oakwood Cemetery.[219]

EMMA ADAMS GEER (c. 1847-1870)
(George W. Adams, Catharine McDonald Adams, Richard McDonald, Maj. Richard, Col. William, William MacDonel)

Emma Adams, the third child of George Washington and Lydia (Fowler) Adams, was born about 1847, in Brunswick, Rensselaer County, New York.[220] She married a Mr. Geer and died in Brunswick on Feb. 5, 1870. She was only 23 years old.[221]

ELLEN "ADDIE" ADAMS MAIN (c. 1854-aft. 1930) AND FAMILY
(George W. Adams, Catharine McDonald Adams, Richard McDonald, Maj. Richard, Col. William, William MacDonel)

Ellen "Addie" Adams,[222] the third child of George Washington and Lydia (Fowler) Adams, was born about 1854 in Brunswick, Rennselaer County, New York.[223]

About 1874, she married George A. Main. He was born in New York about 1852. In 1880, he was employed as a butcher in Troy.[224] They had one child, Hila A. Main, born in 1886.

By 1900, the family had moved to Buffalo, Erie County, New York, where George was employed as a railroad ticket salesman.[225]

They apparently remained in Buffalo to the end of their days. George was working as a clerk for the Great Lakes Transportation Co. in 1920 and as a clerk in a steamship office in 1930. Both George and Ellen died sometime after 1930.

HILA A. MAIN (c. 1854-aft. 1930)
(Ellen Adams Main, George W. Adams, Catharine McDonald Adams, Richard McDonald, Maj. Richard,
 Col. William, William MacDonel)

Hila A. Main, the only child of George A. and Ellen (Adams) Main, was born in New York on Oct. 18, 1866. Her middle name was probably Adams. She graduated from high school and never married.

In 1920, Hila was employed as a clerk with the Great Lakes Transportation Co. in Buffalo, Erie County, New York, the same company for which her father worked. Between 1930 and 1940, she worked as a stenographer for a dry dock company. Julia M. Lusk, age 55, was living with her in 1940, listed as her partner.

Hila lived a very long life. She died in Buffalo in February 1981 at the age of 94.[226]

Chapter 4

ELIZABETH MCDONALD WELLS
(1799 - 1872)
and Her Descendants

Great Great Grandparents: William and Florance MacDonel

Great Grandparents: Col. William McDonald and Unknown First Wife

Grandparents: Maj. Richard McDonald and Margrietje Schamp

Parents: Richard McDonald and Catharine Lansing

Siblings: Richard L., Catharine, Abraham, Lansing, Alanson, George, Jane, Jacob

ELIZABETH MCDONALD (1799 - 1872)
+ Philander Wells (1794-1870)

1. Elizabeth Van Schoonhovan (1824-1871, m. John Benjamin Gale)
2. Catherine J. (1829-1922, m. John Benjamin Gale)
3. Mary J. (c. 1831-aft. 1870)
4. Phebe H. B. (c. 1838-aft. 1865)

Elizabeth McDonald, the second daughter of Richard and Catharine (Lansing) McDonald, was born June 17, 1799, in Lansingburgh, Rensselaer County, New York.[227] She may have been named after her aunt, Elizabeth Lansing Gaston (c. 1775-1857). It is interesting to note that there were Gastons in Somerset County, New Jersey. In fact, it was a Hugh Gaston who bought the former Dr. William McKissack house in Pluckemin from Elias Brown. Dr. McKissack was the son-in-law of Col. William McDonald. His house may well have been Col. William's house originally, the house in which Maj. Richard McDonald grew up.[228]

On Nov. 3, 1823, Elizabeth married Philander Wells, the son of Eleazer and Joanna (Fellows) Wells.[229] He was born June 14, 1794, in New Lebanon Springs, Columbia County, New York, six years older than she.[230] Philander and Elizabeth made their home in Troy, Rensselaer County, New York, where Philander made his living as a banker. He was also treasurer of the Troy and Greenbush Railroad in 1859.[231]

Census records indicate Philander must have retired from his official business about 1860, as no occupation is listed for him. The 1870 census shows him as a retired banker. He possessed real estate valued at $105,000 – quite a sum in those days. His adult children, Catherine and Mary, both in their late 30's, were living with them in 1870.[232]

On Feb. 16, 1866, Philander wrote his Last Will and Testament.[233] He died of angina pectoris on Sept. 26, 1870, aged 76 years, 3 months and 12 days.[234]

Elizabeth McDonald Wells died of diphtheria on Jan. 12, 1872, in Troy, aged 72. She was buried in Oakwood Cemetery in Troy.[235]

Little is known of the two youngest of Philander and Elizabeth's children: Mary J. and Phebe H. B. Both women were living with their parents in Troy in 1865 at the end of the Civil War.[236] Thereafter, Phebe disappears from the records. Mary J. was still living with her parents in 1870, but then she disappears as well.

ELIZABETH VAN SCHOONHOVAN WELLS GALE (1824-1871) AND FAMILY
(Elizabeth McDonald Wells, Richard McDonald, Maj. Richard, Col. William, William MacDonel)

Elizabeth Van Schoonhovan Wells,[237] the eldest child of Philander and Elizabeth (McDonald) Wells, was born Aug. 8, 1824, in Rensselaer County, New York.[238] About 1846, she married John Benjamin Gale, the son of Samuel and Mary (Thompson) Gale.[239]

John was born in Troy, Rensselaer County, on May 9, 1824.[240] He was a lawyer who evidently made a very good living. In 1850, he had real estate valued at $50,000.[241] He was 5'7" tall with dark gray eyes and black hair which turned gray as he aged.[242]

John B. and Elizabeth (Wells) Gale lived in Troy and had three children:
1. Mary E. (c. 1847-bef. 1860)
2. Caroline De Forest (1848-1926, m. Dr. Edward Reynolds Hun)
3. Frederick W. (1850-aft. 1872)

The eldest daughter, Mary E., must have died before 1860 as she does not appear in that census. Her mother, Elizabeth Wells Gale, died fairly young as well, on June 5, 1871, of Bright's Disease,[243] when she was only 46 years old.[244] She was buried in Oakwood Cemetery.

Frederick W. Gale, the only son, was born Mar. 29, 1850, in Troy. He was alive as late as March 1872 when he applied for a passport to travel abroad, but thereafter he disappears from the records.[245]

John B. Gale married again in 1872 to Catherine J. Wells, Elizabeth's younger sister. She was about 43 years old at the time. In 1880, they were still living in Troy, but by 1900 they had moved to Williamstown, Berkshire County, Massachusetts, where John was earning income as a landlord.

John B. Gale died in Williamstown on May 17, 1906, at the age of 82.[246] His second wife, Catherine, died on Dec. 6, 1922, aged 93, and was buried in Oakwood Cemetery in Troy.[247]

CAROLINE DE FOREST GALE HUN (1848-1926) AND FAMILY
(Elizabeth Wells Gale, Elizabeth McDonald Wells, Richard McDonald, Maj. Richard, Col. William,
  William MacDonel)

Caroline De Forest Gale, the middle child of John Benjamin and Elizabeth V. S. (Wells) Gale, was born on Dec. 27, 1848, in Troy, Rensselaer County, New York.[248] She was named after her father's sister-in-law, Caroline De Forest Gale, wife of John Benjamin's brother, Ezra Thompson Gale.[249]

The Gales were descended from Rev. John Eliot (c. 1604-1690), pastor of the First Church of Roxbury, Massachusetts, known to American history as the "Apostle to the Indians" for his pioneering missionary work with the Massachusett Indians.[250] He translated the Bible into the Indian language, the first Bible printed in America.

Caroline De Forest Gale married Dr. Edward Reynolds Hun, the son of Dr. Thomas and Lydia Louisa (Reynolds) Hun, in April 1874.[251]

Dr. Edward R. Hun was born April 17, 1842, in Albany, Albany County, New York.[252] He received his A.B. from Harvard College in 1863[253] and graduated from Columbia University College of Physicians and Surgeons in 1866.[254] He then traveled to Europe to further his studies in London and Paris.

Upon his return to the States, Dr. Hun established a general practice in Albany. He had a distinguished medical career. From 1868-1873, he was appointed special pathologist to the New York State Lunatic Asylum at Utica. In 1875, he was secretary of the Medical Society of the State of New York, as well as the chair of nervous diseases at the Albany Medical College. Dr. Hun made various contributions to medical journals and was the author of *Trichina-Spiralis* (1869), *Pulse of the Insane* (1870) and *Hæmatoma Auris* (1870).[255]

> He was greatly interested in the advance of medicine and in new scientific methods and appliances. He possessed unusual qualities of mind and great quickness of perception in detecting the characteristics of disease. His nature was an ardent and sympathetic one.[256]

Sadly, Dr. Hun's health began to fail him after being involved in a serious accident "while driving on the Troy road."[257] For several years he was unable to continue his practice. He died of inflammation of the lungs in Stamford, Fairfield County, Connecticut, on March 14, 1880.[258] He was only 37 years old.

Caroline Gale Hun lived as a widow for another 46 years. She died in Albany on Dec. 13, 1926, at the age of 77. Both Edward and Caroline were laid to rest in Albany Rural Cemetery, Menands, Albany County, New York.[259]

Dr. Edward Reynolds and Caroline De Forest (Gale) Hun had four children:
1. Lydia Louise (1875-1975, m. Frederick Williams Kelley)
2. Elizabeth Gale (1876-1889)
3. John Gale (1877-1945, m. Leslie Stafford Crawford)
4. Katherine (1880-1978, m. William Law Learned Peltz)

Elizabeth Gale Hun, the second child of Dr. Edward and Caroline Hun, was born Nov. 5, 1876, in Albany. She only lived to the age of 12, passing in Albany on Oct. 15, 1889.[260]

LYDIA LOUISE HUN KELLEY (1875-1975) AND FAMILY
(Caroline Gale Hun, Elizabeth Wells Gale, Elizabeth McDonald Wells, Richard McDonald, Maj. Richard,
  Col. William, William MacDonel)

Lydia Louise Hun, the eldest child of Dr. Edward Reynolds and Caroline De Forest (Gale) Hun, was born July 8, 1875, in Albany, Albany County, New York.[261] She was named after her paternal grandmother, Lydia Louisa Reynolds Hun.

On Apr. 29, 1903, in Albany, when she was 27 years old, Lydia married Frederick Williams Kelley, the son of lumber dealer James Blinn and Alice (Williams) Kelley of Toledo, Lucas County, Ohio.[262]

Born in Albany on Dec. 15, 1870,[263] Frederick W. Kelley studied mechanical engineering and graduated in 1893 from Cornell University.[264] While at Cornell, he was a member of Psi Upsilon and Sphinx Head, as well as a member of the Varsity Crew Squad.[265]

Frederick was president of the Helderberg Cement Company, which he consolidated with the Security Cement and Lime Company forming the North American Cement Company in 1915. [266] Over the course of his life, Frederick was president of the Albany Chamber of Commerce and the Portland Cement Association. He served as president of the board of the Albany Hospital and vice president of the National Commercial Bank and Trust Company. He was also instrumental in helping to re-open Howe's Caverns in Schoharie County, New York, a favorite destination of spelunkers and the second most visited natural attraction in the state in 1932.[267]

Frederick and Lydia (Hun) Kelley had two children:
1. Alice Williams (1904-2003, m. Arthur Brooks Harlow)
2. Frederick Williams Jr. (1908-1966, m. Aubrey McKowan)

In August of 1924, passport applications reveal that Frederick and his 16-year-old son, Frederick Jr., toured Great Britain, France, Germany and Italy.[268]

About 1928, Frederick Sr. suffered a stroke, which left him unable to walk and confined to a wheelchair. He died of asthma at the age of 61 on Sept. 19, 1932, at his summer home in Altamont, Albany County, New York.[269]

Lydia Hun Kelley lived for another 42+ years following her husband's death. She set a record for longevity in this branch of the McDonald family tree, succumbing to pneumonia on Aug. 14, 1975, at the age of 100 years, 1 month and 6 days.[270] Both she and Frederick were buried in Albany Rural Cemetery, Menands, Albany County, New York.[271]

ALICE WILLIAMS KELLEY HARLOW (1904-2003) AND FAMILY
(Lydia Hun Kelley, Caroline Gale Hun, Elizabeth Wells Gale, Elizabeth McDonald Wells, Richard McDonald,
 Maj. Richard, Col. William, William MacDonel)

Alice Williams Kelley, the eldest child of Frederick W. Sr. and Lydia L. (Hun) Kelley, was born Nov. 26, 1904, in Albany, Albany County, New York.[272] She married Arthur Brooks Harlow, better known as A. Brooks, the son of Dr. George Arthur and Genevieve (Hancock) Harlow.[273]

A. Brooks Harlow was born in Milwaukee, Milwaukee County, Wisconsin, on Dec. 1, 1901.[274] A 1925 graduate of Harvard University, he went into the life insurance business. In 1941, he was working for the Mutual Benefit Life Insurance Co. at 135 Broadway in New York City.[275]

During World War II, A. Brooks served as captain in the 9th regiment of the New York National Guard. He and Alice were living in Darien, Fairfield County, Connecticut at the time.[276]

A. Brooks Sr. died on July 22, 1994, in Juno Beach, Palm Beach County, Florida, aged 92. His wife, Alice, died in Juno Beach on Jan. 5, 2003, aged 98.[277] Both were buried in Albany Rural Cemetery, Menands, Albany County, New York.[278]

Arthur Brooks Sr. and Alice (Kelley) Harlow had a son: Arthur Brooks Harlow Jr.

ARTHUR BROOKS HARLOW JR. (1934-2014) AND FAMILY
(Alice Kelley Harlow, Lydia Hun Kelley, Caroline Gale Hun, Elizabeth Wells Gale, Elizabeth McDonald
 Wells, Richard McDonald, Maj. Richard, Col. William, William MacDonel)

Arthur Brooks Harlow Jr., the son of Arthur Brooks Harlow Sr. and Alice W. (Kelley) Harlow, was born June 13, 1934, in Stamford, Fairfield County, Connecticut.[279] He attended Fay School (a boarding school in Southborough, Massachusetts), Groton School (a college preparatory boarding school in Groton, Massachusetts), and Trinity College in Hartford, Connecticut (Class of 1957). While at Trinity, he was a member of the Alpha Delta Phi Fraternity and captain of the squash team.

On June 20, 1969, Arthur Brooks Jr. married Miriam Van Dyck "Mimi" Baxter, who was born Apr. 28, 1933, in Detroit, Wayne County, Michigan. She was a 1954 graduate of the University of Michigan and a member of Kappa Alpha Theta sorority.[280] Arthur Brooks Jr. was Master of the Rectory School in Pomfret, Connecticut, at the time.[281]

Arthur Brooks Jr. and Miriam (Baxter) Harlow had three children:
1. Alice (m. Unknown Ronconi)
2. Elizabeth (m. Unknown Robinson)
3. Arthur Brooks III[282]

In 1967, A. Brooks Jr. became an administrative assistant at Fay School. He was promoted to headmaster in 1969 and served in that capacity until he retired in 1988.

On Dec. 26, 2010, Miriam died in St. Augustine, St. Johns County, Florida, at the age of 77.[283] Her husband, A. Brooks Jr. , followed her on Apr. 15, 2014, in St. Augustine.[284] He was 79 years old.

FREDERICK WILLIAMS KELLEY JR. (1908-1966) AND FAMILY
(Lydia Hun Kelley, Caroline Gale Hun, Elizabeth Wells Gale, Elizabeth McDonald Wells, Richard McDonald, Maj. Richard, Col. William, William MacDonel)

Frederick Williams Kelley Jr., the second child of Frederick W. Sr. and Lydia L. (Hun) Kelley, was born Jan. 18, 1908, in Albany, Albany County, New York.[285] He married Aubrey McKowan, daughter of Henry A. and Evah Mae (Cartwright) McKowan. Aubrey was born Oct. 3, 1910, in British Columbia, Canada.[286] Like his father, Frederick Jr. was a graduate of Cornell University in mechanical engineering (Class of 1929). He was a member of the Varsity Crew Squad and the Officers Club.[287]

In 1940, Frederick and Aubrey were living in Catskill, Greene County, New York. He was working as a researcher for a cement plant.

Frederick W. Jr. and Aubrey (McKowan) Kelley had three children:
1. Frederick W. III
2. Diane K. (m. Unknown Fenton)
3. Lydia E.

Frederick W. Jr. died on Feb. 13, 1966, in Loudonville, Albany County, New York, at the age of 58. Aubrey died on May 15, 1994, in Loudonville, at the age of 83.[288] Both were buried in Albany Rural Cemetery, Menands, Albany County, New York.[289]

JOHN GALE HUN (1877-1945) AND FAMILY
(Caroline Gale Hun, Elizabeth Wells Gale, Elizabeth McDonald Wells, Richard McDonald, Maj. Richard, Col. William, William MacDonel)

John Gale Hun, the second child of Dr. Edward Reynolds and Caroline De Forest (Gale) Hun, was born Nov. 21, 1877, in Albany, Albany County, New York.[290] He attended Albany Boys' Academy and Williams College, where he earned his B.A. in 1899. In 1903, he received a Ph.D. from John Hopkins University.[291] That same year, in the fall, he began teaching mathematics at Princeton University in Mercer County, New Jersey. Little did John know that the home of his McDonald ancestors, Col. William and Maj. Richard McDonald, was just about 22 miles north of Princeton, in Pluckemin, Somerset County, New Jersey.[292]

On June 26, 1906, in Westfield, Hampden County, Massachusetts, John married Leslie Stafford Crawford, the daughter of Rev. Lyndon Smith and Susan Van Vranken (Doolittle) Crawford.[293] Leslie was born in Smyrna, Turkey, on May 1, 1881. Her father was doing missionary work there at the time.[294]

John was the author of several mathematics textbooks including, *The Elements of Plane and Spherical Trigonometry* (1911), co-authored with Charles Ranald MacInnes.[295]

In 1914, John founded and served as headmaster of the Princeton Math School, which was renamed the Hun School of Princeton in 1920, a private secondary boarding school.[296]

John Gale and Leslie (Crawford) Hun had three children:
1. Leslie Crawford (1907-1962, m. Edward Shippen Morris)
2. Elizabeth Gale (1909-1967, m. Maj. Robert Gordon McAllen)
3. Carolyn Gale (b. abt. 1913, m. Francis Turquand Miles)

John died on Sept. 15, 1945, at Mercer Hospital in Trenton, Mercer County, New Jersey. He was 67 years old. His wife, Leslie, died in Princeton on June 21, 1964.[297] She was 83. Both were buried in Albany Rural Cemetery, Menands, Albany County, New York.[298]

LESLIE CRAWFORD HUN MORRIS (1907-1962) AND FAMILY
(John Gale Hun, Caroline Gale Hun, Elizabeth Wells Gale, Elizabeth McDonald Wells, Richard McDonald, Maj. Richard, Col. William, William MacDonel)

Leslie Crawford Hun, the eldest child of John Gale and Leslie Stafford (Crawford) Hun, was born Oct. 21, 1907, in Princeton, Mercer County, New Jersey.[299]

In 1932, Leslie married Edward Shippen Morris, the son of Roland Sletor and Augusta Shippen (West) Morris.[300] Edward was born in Philadelphia, Philadelphia County, Pennsylvania, on Valentine's Day, Feb. 14, 1906.[301] He was a descendant of Capt. Samuel Morris, the founder of the First City Troop of Philadelphia in the American Revolution.[302] His father, Roland Sletor Morris, was a lawyer and a graduate of Princeton University, who specialized in corporation law. Roland was a delegate to the Democratic National Convention of 1904, 1908 and 1912. From 1908 – 1916, he was chairman of the Democratic Finance Committee of Pennsylvania. On July 20, 1917, he was appointed Ambassador to Japan by President Woodrow Wilson, a position he held until the inauguration of Republican President Warren G. Harding.[303]

Edward Shippen Morris attended the Phillips Exeter Academy in Exeter, New Hampshire, and was a 1928 graduate of Princeton University.[304] He practiced law in Philadelphia for many years and was a lifelong Democrat. He served as Deputy Attorney General for the state of Pennsylvania during the administration of Gov. George Earle.

Edward was also very active in his community. He was a member of the board of several organizations including St. Stephens Church in Philadelphia, the Big Brothers Association, and the Philadelphia Civic Opera Company. He was also trustee, treasurer and counsel of the Burd School in Philadelphia and a trustee for The Hun School of Princeton. He was a director for the World Affairs Council and a member of the national board of the Foreign Policy Association.[305]

Edward Shippen Morris died in Philadelphia on May 15, 1959, at the age of 53. Several years before his death, he had an operation requiring the removal of his vocal cords. He had to learn to speak all over again, yet he "never lost his optimism and cheerful personality."[306]

Leslie Hun Morris passed away in Philadelphia on July 10, 1962.[307] She was only 54. Both Edward and Leslie were buried in Laurel Hill Cemetery in Philadelphia.[308]

Edward Shippen and Leslie (Hun) Morris had one son, Roland Morris.

ROLAND MORRIS (1933-Living)
(Leslie Hun Morris, John Gale Hun, Caroline Gale Hun, Elizabeth Wells Gale, Elizabeth McDonald Wells, Richard McDonald, Maj. Richard, Col. William, William MacDonel)

Roland Morris, the son of Edward Shippen and Leslie (Hun) Morris, was born in 1933 in Pennsylvania. Like his father, he attended Phillips Exeter Academy, then graduated from Princeton University (Class of 1955). While in college, he was editor of the *Daily Princetonian* and a member of Ivy Club.[309]

Roland married Sally Jean Fageol, the daughter of Robley D. and Geraldine (Marlatt) Fageol of Detroit, Michigan, on Jan. 29, 1955, at Trinity Episcopal Church in Princeton, Mercer County, New Jersey.[310]

In 1960, Roland graduated from the University of Pennsylvania Law School. He joined the law firm of Duane Morris, LLP, specializing in the areas of administrative, antitrust, and healthcare law and economic litigation. He has appeared for clients before the supreme courts of New Jersey and Pennsylvania, as well as the Supreme Court of the United States.

Like his father, Roland has been involved in many civic and charitable activities. He served as president of the Big Brothers Association of Philadelphia from 1975-1987, director of the Citizens Crime Commission of Philadelphia, board member of United Way and the Salvation Army, and trustee of Thomas Jefferson University.[311]

ELIZABETH GALE HUN MCALLEN (1909-1967) AND FAMILY
(John Gale Hun, Caroline Gale Hun, Elizabeth Wells Gale, Elizabeth McDonald Wells, Richard McDonald, Maj. Richard, Col. William, William MacDonel)

Elizabeth Gale Hun, the middle child of John Gale and Leslie Stafford (Crawford) Hun, was born July 9, 1909, in Albany, Albany County, New York.[312] She attended Sweet Briar College (Class of 1932), a women's liberal arts college located in Sweet Briar, Virginia, in the foothills of the Blue Ridge Mountains.[313]

In 1931, Elizabeth married Robert Gordon McAllen, the son of William J. and Clementine (Gordon) McAllen. Robert was born on July 6, 1907, in Chicago, Cook County, Illinois.[314] He received a B.S. in physics from Princeton University and was a member of Phi Beta Kappa.

In 1934, Robert was appointed assistant principal of the Hun Senior School. He stayed in that role until the outbreak of World War II. He joined the army, held the rank of major, and served on Gen. Douglas McArthur's staff in Tokyo.[315] After the war, Robert became headmaster of The Hun School from 1946-1949.

Maj. McAllen died May 28, 1971, when he was 63 years old.[316] His wife, Elizabeth, died Sept. 13, 1967, at age 58. They are buried at Trinity All Saints Cemetery, Princeton, New Jersey.[317]

Maj. Robert Gordon and Elizabeth (Hun) McAllen had two children:

1. Elizabeth Gordon (b. abt. 1934, m. Unknown Baker)
2. Susan Hun (1936-2005, m. Alfred H. Turner Jr.)

ELIZABETH GORDON MCALLEN BAKER (c. 1934-Living)

(Elizabeth Hun McAllen, John Gale Hun, Caroline Gale Hun, Elizabeth Wells Gale, Elizabeth McDonald
  Wells, Richard McDonald, Maj. Richard, Col. William, William MacDonel)

Elizabeth Gordon McAllen, the eldest child of Maj. Robert Gordon and Elizabeth (Hun) McAllen, was born in
October 1933 in New Jersey.[318] Known as Gordon McAllen Baker, she studied art, painting, drawing and
etching at Colby-Sawyer College, graduating with the Class of 1953. She now lives in Lexington, Virginia.[319]

SUSAN HUN MCALLEN TURNER (1936-2005) AND FAMILY

(Elizabeth Hun McAllen, John Gale Hun, Caroline Gale Hun, Elizabeth Wells Gale, Elizabeth McDonald
  Wells, Richard McDonald, Maj. Richard, Col. William, William MacDonel)

Susan Hun McAllen, the second child of Maj. Robert Gordon and Elizabeth (Hun) McAllen, was born Feb. 11,
1936, in Princeton, Mercer County, New Jersey. She graduated from Miss Fine's School in Princeton in 1953
and Wheaton College in Norton, Massachusetts in 1957.

She married Alfred H. Turner Jr. They owned and operated the Keene Valley Hardware in Keene Valley, New
York.[320] They had two children: Katherine (m. Kevin Casler) and Eleanor (m. Daniel O'Connell).

Susan's passion was bobsledding. She was secretary-treasurer of the Hurricane Bobsled Club and in 1980
became chairman of the Olympic Bobsled Scoreboard for the XIII Winter Olympic Games in Lake Placid, New
York. In 1983, she was first vice-president of the U.S. Bobsled and Skeleton Federation. She also holds the
distinction of being the first woman to become an internationally licensed FIBT jury member (Fédération
Internationale de Bobsleigh et de Tobogganing). From 2003-2004, she served as race secretary for all
international bobsled and skeleton races held at Lake Placid.[321]

Susan died on April 5, 2005, in Saranac Lake, New York. She was 69. She is survived by her husband, children
and three grandchildren.

CAROLYN GALE HUN MILES (c. 1913-unknown)

(John Gale Hun, Caroline Gale Hun, Elizabeth Wells Gale, Elizabeth McDonald Wells, Richard McDonald,
  Maj. Richard, Col. William, William MacDonel)

Carolyn Gale Hun, the youngest child of John Gale and Leslie Stafford (Crawford) Hun, was born in New York
City about 1913.[322] She graduated from high school and married Francis Turquand Miles, a chemist who
graduated from Princeton University with the class of 1931.[323] Born on July 10, 1909, in Princeton, Francis was
the son of Lewis Wardlaw and Katherine (Stockton) Miles.[324] Francis was named after his grandfather,
Dr. Francis Turquand Miles (1827-1903), an anatomy professor at the University of Charleston, who, when the
Civil War broke out, joined the Confederacy as captain of Company E in the 1st South Carolina Infantry

Battalion. In 1862, he was wounded at the Battle of Secessionville, repelling a Union attempt to capture Charleston. Later in the war he was transferred to a medical unit to perform surgery.[325]

Francis Turquand Miles, the younger, and his wife Carolyn Gale (Hun) Miles, had a daughter Leslie C. H. Miles, born about 1938 in Alabama.[326] Francis died on Oct. 10, 1994, in Lexington, Middlesex County, Massachusetts, at the age of 65.[327] His wife's death date is unknown. She was alive and living in Vienna, Austria, in 1964, when her mother died.[328]

KATHERINE HUN PELTZ (1880-1978) AND FAMILY
(Caroline Gale Hun, Elizabeth Wells Gale, Elizabeth McDonald Wells, Richard McDonald, Maj. Richard,
  Col. William, William MacDonel)

Katherine Hun, the youngest of four children of Dr. Edward Reynolds and Caroline De Forest (Gale) Hun, was born Jan. 21, 1880, in Stamford, Fairfield County, Connecticut.[329] She graduated from high school and on Apr. 27, 1907, in Albany, New York, married William Law Learned Peltz, the son of John DeWitt and Mary Marvin (Learned) Peltz.[330]

Interestingly, William Law Learned Peltz was a descendant of Tjerick DeWitt, who emigrated from Holland and settled in Kingston, Ulster County, New York, in 1656. Little did he know that he had McDonald cousins who also married into the DeWitt family, descended from the immigrant Tjerick DeWitt.[331] Specifically, it was Mary Antoinette MacDonald, the daughter of Mayor Richard MacDonald of New Brunswick, New Jersey, who married Rep. David Miller DeWitt of Kingston. Mayor Richard MacDonald was the son of Col. George McDonald of Somerset County, New Jersey, who was, in turn, the son of Revolutionary War veteran, Maj. Richard McDonald, the ancestor of Katherine Hun Peltz.[332]

William Law Learned Peltz was a lawyer with an independent practice in Albany. Born May 27, 1882, in Albany, he attended Albany Academy, Yale University (Class of 1904), and the Albany Law School, Union University (graduating in 1906). At one time he was director of the Albany Historical Society and president of the Albany Academy Alumni Association.[333]

William died in Selkirk on Mar. 26, 1961. He was 78. His wife, Katherine, died on Feb. 1, 1978, in Williamstown, Berkshire County, Massachusetts. She was 98. Both were buried in Albany Rural Cemetery, Menands, Albany County, New York.[334]

William Law Learned and Katherine (Hun) Peltz had four children:
1. Caroline (1908-2007, m. Chester B. Kerr, Dr. Edward Scott Goodwin, Dr. Paul Schultze)
2. William Learned (1909-2003, m. Margaret Ruth Adams)
3. Mary Learned (1914-2005, m. Dr. Theodore Burg Russell, Lewis Perry Jr.)
4. Philip (1915-2001, m. Elizabeth Davenport Hooper)

CAROLINE PELTZ KERR GOODWIN SCHULTZE (1908-2007) AND FAMILY
(Katherine Hun Peltz, Caroline Gale Hun, Elizabeth Wells Gale, Elizabeth McDonald Wells, Richard McDonald, Maj. Richard, Col. William, William MacDonel)

Caroline Peltz, the eldest child of William Law Learned and Katherine (Hun) Peltz, was born Feb. 19, 1908, in Albany, Albany County, New York. She graduated from the Albany Academy for Girls and went on to study art in Boston.

About 1938, when she was about 30, she married Chester Brooks Kerr, the son of Chester K. and Mary (Seymour) Kerr.[335] Chester and Caroline had two children: John S. Kerr II and Philip Kerr.

Born in Norwalk, Fairfield County, Connecticut, on Aug. 5, 1913,[336] Chester Brooks Kerr graduated from Yale University with the Class of 1936.[337] His roommate was John Hersey, who became a World War II correspondent and winner of the Pulitzer Prize for his novel, *A Bell for Adano.*

Chester was editor of the Yale University Press from 1939-1979 and president of Ticknor & Fields, a Houghton Mifflin Company. He was elected to the Publishers Hall of Fame in 1986. The marriage to Caroline ended in divorce.[338]

About 1943, Caroline married Dr. Edward Scott Goodwin, "a physician for children."[339] They had a son, George Goodwin. Dr. Goodwin was born Oct. 12, 1896, in Glens Falls, Warren County, New York, the son of Scott DuMont and Sarah Coffin (Waite) Goodwin. He died on Apr. 11, 1979, at the age of 82.[340]

After her second husband died, Caroline married, thirdly, Dr. Paul Schultze.

Caroline lived a long, long life, and was active with the Albany Fresh Air Guild, St. Peter's Episcopal Church, the Junior Friday Morning Club and the University Club. She passed away at the age of 99 on May 11, 2007, in Troy, Rensselaer County, New York.[341] She was buried with her second husband, Dr. Edward Scott Goodwin, in Albany Rural Cemetery in Menands, Albany County, New York.[342]

PHILIP KERR (1940-Living) AND FAMILY
(Caroline Peltz Kerr, Katherine Hun Peltz, Caroline Gale Hun, Elizabeth Wells Gale, Elizabeth McDonald Wells, Richard McDonald, Maj. Richard, Col. William, William MacDonel)

Philip Kerr, the son of Caroline Peltz by her first husband, Chester B. Kerr, was born in New York City on Apr. 9, 1940. He attended Westminster School in Simsbury, Connecticut, then went on to Harvard University (Class of 1963) and further training at the London Academy of Music and Dramatic Art in England.[343]

An accomplished actor, Philip appeared on Broadway in *Macbeth*, starring Christopher Plummer and Glenda Jackson (1988), *Otherwise Engaged* (directed by Harold Pinter), and *Three Sisters* (directed by William Ball). In 1970, he played at Carnegie Hall in *Hamlet*, starring Dame Judith Anderson in the title role.[344] Off Broadway he applied his talents to such reputable companies as Manhattan Theatre Club, Roundabout Theatre and CSC Repertory. Regionally, he played Robert E. Lee in a production of *Appomattox* at the Guthrie Theatre in Minneapolis, among many others.[345]

From 1984-2012, Philip taught theatre and directed plays at the University of Michigan at Ann Arbor. He was instrumental in developing the Department of Theatre and Drama's B.F.A. program. He has also taught master classes at American Conservatory Theatre in San Francisco, Indiana State University, College of the Sequoias and Bennington College.[346]

In 1983, Philip married Sarah-Jane Gwillim, a British television and stage actress who also taught at the University of Michigan. She appeared on Broadway in the 1980's in *Macbeth*, *Major Barbara* and *Saint Joan*.[347] She is the daughter of British character actor, Jack Gwillim, and sister of actor David Gwillim.

Philip and Sarah-Jane have four children. They are enjoying retirement on their farm in upstate New York.[348]

WILLIAM LEARNED PELTZ (1909-2003) AND FAMILY
(Katherine Hun Peltz, Caroline Gale Hun, Elizabeth Wells Gale, Elizabeth McDonald Wells, Richard
 McDonald, Maj. Richard, Col. William, William MacDonel)

William Learned Peltz, the second child of William Law Learned and Katherine (Hun) Peltz, was born on Feb. 11, 1909, in Albany, Albany County, New York. He attended Albany Academy and Phillips Exeter Academy before graduating from Yale University with the Class of 1931.

While at Yale, William worked on the *Yale Daily News*, the freshman yearbook, and the 1931 Class Book. He was a member of Alpha Delta Phi and The Whiffenpoofs, because of his ability to yodel.[349] After graduation, he took a year to travel through Europe and the Middle East. Upon his return, he entered Yale Medical School, transferring to Harvard Medical School for the final two years, graduating in 1936.[350]

William became a psychiatrist. He married Margaret Ruth Adams, the daughter of Mason Tyler and Juliette (Hubbell) Adams, on Jan. 29, 1938, in Exeter, Rockingham County, New Hampshire.[351] Margaret was born on Sept. 26, 1912, in Morristown, Morris County, New Jersey.[352] Her stepfather, Lewis Perry Sr. (1877-1970), was the headmaster of the Phillips Exeter Academy in Exeter, Rockingham, New Hampshire, for many years.[353]

During World War II, Dr. Peltz applied his medical knowledge and skill to the Yale Hospital Unit, which became the 39th General Hospital, then served for two years in New Zealand and one year in Saipan. While in New Zealand he was transferred to the Psychiatric Service. At the time of his honorable discharge from duty, he had attained the rank of major.

After the war, William and his family moved to the Philadelphia area, where he continued to study and train in psychiatry and psychoanalysis. During the Korean Conflict, he served in both Korea and Okinawa as a civilian consultant in psychiatry to the U.S. Army Surgeon General.

For 25 years, William practiced psychiatry at the Institute of Pennsylvania Hospital. He was also professor of clinical psychiatry at the University of Pennsylvania School of Medicine.

In 1970, he and his wife, Margaret, moved to Manchester, Bennington County, Vermont, where he continued to practice psychiatry part-time before he retired completely in 1984, at which time they moved to Lambert's Cove on Martha's Vineyard, Massachusetts. William enjoyed painting the local scenery: sailing ships, skiers and the natural surroundings. Vineyard galleries featured several of his works.[354]

William's wife, Margaret Ruth Adams Peltz, was a professional monologist. She performed for more than 50 years in the U.S. and Canada. She died on Jan. 23, 1998, in Oak Bluffs on Martha's Vineyard, at the age of 85.[355]

The good doctor died on Sept. 23, 2003, in Salem, Essex County, Massachusetts, at the age of 94.[356] He and his wife were buried in Lamberts Cove Cemetery, West Tisbury, Dukes County, Massachusetts.[357]

They are survived by three sons – Mason, William and Thomas – and five grandchildren – Samantha, Kate, Daniel, Jennifer and Lauren.[358]

WILLIAM HUN PELTZ (1947-Living) AND FAMILY
(William L. Peltz, Katherine Hun Peltz, Caroline Gale Hun, Elizabeth Wells Gale, Elizabeth McDonald Wells, Richard McDonald, Maj. Richard, Col. William, William MacDonel)

William Hun "Bill" Peltz, the middle son of Dr. William Learned and Margaret Ruth (Adams) Peltz, was born Sept. 22, 1947, in Philadelphia, Philadelphia County, Pennsylvania. He attended Haverford School until 1962, then graduated from Millbrook School in Millbrook, New York, in 1965. His studies continued at Malvern College in Malvern, Worcestershire, England, in 1965 and 1966. In 1971, he graduated from Denver University in Denver, Colorado, with a degree in biology. From 1970-1971, he studied at the University of Pennsylvania in Philadelphia, and in 1976, he received his M. Ed. in educational administration from Teachers College, Columbia University, New York.[359]

On June 30, 1973, in Quaker Hill, New York, Bill married Neville Joanna Farquharson Bryan, daughter of Judge Frederick van Peltz Bryan and Denise Bryan.[360]

Bill was a teacher and administrator at Greenwich Academy (Greenwich, CT) from 1971-2009, while teaching at the Selwyn School (Denton, TX) from 1980-1981. He is now Director of Soar For Success, LLC, a tutoring/high stakes exam prep business, and co-owner of Larus Institute Public Safety Candidate Prep, LLP, which prepares candidates for entry level career fire service exams and interviews.[361]

Bill and Neville Peltz have two children:
1. Daniel Learned (b. 1976, m. Melissa D'Louhy)
2. Jennifer Bryan (b. 1980, m. Brian McCurley)[362]

Son Daniel was born Jan. 16, 1976, in Greenwich, Fairfield County, Connecticut. He is a stay-at-home dad and sells products on eBay. His wife, Melissa, better known as Missy, is executive creative director at Anthropologie, a lifestyle brand that celebrates art, style, design and discovery, operating over 200 stores worldwide.[363] Daniel and Missy live in Philadelphia with their two children, Grey, age 7, and Sidney, age 5.

Daughter Jennifer was born in Greenwich on May 23, 1980. She and her husband, Brian, have a son, William, age 2. The McCurleys left Los Angeles, where Brian worked in the production end of the Hollywood business.

They now live in Londonderry, Rockingham County, New Hampshire. Jennifer is employed as visual merchandising associate for American Girl at Mattel and Brian just became a real estate agent.[364]

⟨───⫘───⟩

MARY LEARNED PELTZ RUSSELL PERRY (1914-2005) AND FAMILY
(Katherine Hun Peltz, Caroline Gale Hun, Elizabeth Wells Gale, Elizabeth McDonald Wells, Richard McDonald, Maj. Richard, Col. William, William MacDonel)

Mary Learned Peltz, the third child of William Law Learned and Katherine (Hun) Peltz, was born on Dec. 16, 1914, in Albany, Albany County, New York.[365] She graduated from high school and married Dr. Theodore Burg "Ted" Russell, the son of John Burg and Eveleen (Kane) Russell, on June 24, 1939, in Selkirk, Albany County, New York. Ted was born on Sept. 23, 1903, in New York City.[366] He graduated from Princeton University and then attended the College of Physicians and Surgeons at Columbia University. He engaged in general practice and internal medicine at Bellevue, Columbia-Presbyterian and the Veterans Administration Hospital in the Bronx.

During World War II, Ted served as a Navy physician in the South Pacific, achieving the rank of commander. After the war, he practiced medicine in Ann Arbor, Michigan.[367]

Ted and Mary (Peltz) Russell had three daughters:
1. Mary Kane (1940-Living, m. Richard Booth White)
2. Katherine (1943-2008, m. Benno C. Schmidt Jr.)
3. Phoebe (1947-Living, m. Lewis Perry MacAdams Jr., Ron Ozuna) [368]

Ted and Mary's marriage ended in divorce.

In 1965, Mary Learned Peltz Russell married Lewis Perry Jr., the son of Lewis Sr. and Margaret (Hubbell) Perry. Lewis Sr. was the headmaster of Phillips Exeter Academy in Exeter, New Hampshire.[369] Lewis Jr. was born Mar. 4, 1913, in Williamstown, Berkshire County, Massachusetts. He was highly educated, having attended Milton Academy, Phillips Exeter Academy, Harvard University and Oxford University.

Lewis Jr. was also a veteran of World War II, having served in the U.S. Navy from 1943-1946 as an air combat intelligence officer aboard the *USS Santee* (ACV-29), an escort carrier. He was involved in several combat operations including the Battle of Leyte Gulf.[370]

Lewis taught English at the Lawrenceville School from 1938-1958, and from 1958-1978 he was headmaster of the Fountain Valley School in Colorado Springs, Colorado. Beloved both as teacher and headmaster, Lewis's passions included literature, theatre and sports. He coached soccer, loved to watch football, skied and played golf.[371]

Mary Learned Peltz Russell Perry died on July 13, 2005, at the age of 90.[372] Her first husband, Dr. Ted Russell, died at the Columbia Presbyterian Medical Center in New York City on Dec. 30, 1970, aged 67.[373] He was buried in Green-Wood Cemetery, Brooklyn, Kings County, New York.[374] Her second husband, Lewis Perry Jr., died in his sleep on Aug. 7, 2010, in Colorado Springs. He was 97.[375]

MARY KANE RUSSELL WHITE (1940-Living) AND FAMILY

(Mary Peltz Russell, Katherine Hun Peltz, Caroline Gale Hun, Elizabeth Wells Gale, Elizabeth McDonald Wells, Richard McDonald, Maj. Richard, Col. William, William MacDonel)

Mary Kane Russell, the eldest child of Dr. Theodore Burg and Mary (Peltz) Russell, was born Aug. 26, 1940, in New York City. She now lives in New Canaan, Fairfield County, Connecticut. Kane graduated from Emma Willard School in 1958. She attended Wheaton College before graduating from Sarah Lawrence College in 1995. She is a member of the First Presbyterian Church in New Canaan, is sustaining member of the Garden Club of America in New Canaan and is involved with Landmark Worldwide.[376]

She married Richard Booth "Dick" White Sr., the son of Frank Kiggins and Doris (Booth) White, on Dec. 9, 1961. They were married for 56 years.

Richard was born Aug. 26, 1930, in New York City.[377] He graduated from Yale University in 1952 with degrees in English and psychology. He then spent three years with the United States Marine Corps as a 1st lieutenant of infantry and as an intelligence specialist attached to the C.I.A.[378]

In 1955, Richard joined the advertising firm of BBDO (Batten, Barton, Durstine & Osborn), New York City, eventually rising through the ranks to become the company's executive vice president, board member and chairman of the executive committee. He had senior management responsibility for the corporate accounts of General Electric, Scott Paper, Campbell Soup and Gillette, among others.

From 1984-1998, Richard was senior director and partner of Spencer Stuart & Associates, New York City.[379]

Apart from his business pursuits, Richard was also actively involved in civic affairs. He was a member of the New Canaan Town Council, belonged to the First Presbyterian Church of New Canaan, and served on the Board of Directors of VITAM, the Stamford Symphony Orchestra and the board of the Madison Square Boys and Girls Club of New York City. In addition, Dick was active in elder care issues in New Canaan, serving on the boards of the New Canaan Inn and Waveney Care Center.[380]

Richard passed away on Apr. 26, 2014, at the age of 83.[381]

Richard and Mary Kane (Russell) White had four children:
1. Katherine Learned (1964, m. Michael Thomas Marsland)
2. Richard Booth Jr. (1966 –1992)[382]
3. Anne Tristram (c. 1970, m. David J. Collard Jr.)
4. Leslie (1973, m. Michael Rolf Siek)[383]

KATHERINE LEARNED WHITE MARSLAND (1964-Living) AND FAMILY
(Mary Kane Russell White, Mary Peltz Russell, Katherine Hun Peltz, Caroline Gale Hun, Elizabeth Wells
  Gale, Elizabeth McDonald Wells, Richard McDonald, Maj. Richard, Col. William, William MacDonel)

Katherine Learned "Kate" White, the eldest child of Richard Booth and Mary Kane (Russell) White, was born May 5, 1964, in New York, New York. She was named after her maternal great grandparents, William Law Learned and Katherine (Hun) Peltz.[384]

Katherine graduated from Phillip Academy in 1982 and received her B.A. in psychology from Fairfield University. She completed her Ph.D. in psychology at Yale University in 2005. Dr. Marsland is now an associate professor in the psychology department at Southern Connecticut State University where she researches early socioemotional development, childcare policy, and early childhood education.[385] In addition, she is affiliate faculty at the Yale Zigler Center in Child Development and Social Policy. Kate serves on the Board of Education in Branford and sits on the boards of Branford Cares and the Branford Early Childhood Collaborative as well as on the advisory council for the Gessell Institute of Child Development.[386]

Katherine married Michael Marsland in 1992. Michael graduated from Branford High School in Branford, New Haven County, Connecticut, in 1968, then attended Quinnipiac College and Paier College of Art in Hamden, New Haven County, before he transferred to Charter Oak State College, where he majored in art history and photography. He perfected his professional photography skills in San Francisco at the Fairmont Hotel, the Yale Art Gallery and the British Art Gallery.[387]

Since 1987, Michael has been the University Photographer for Yale University. Marsland has photographed many famous people over the years including Presidents George H. W. Bush, George W. Bush, and Bill Clinton, actress Julie Andrews, British Prime Minister Tony Blair, actor Paul Newman and singers Paul Simon and Paul McCartney.[388]

Michael and Katherine (White) Marsland have a daughter, Sarah Booth (b. 2000), who is a ballerina with the New Haven Ballet.[389]

LESLIE WHITE-SIEK (1973-Living) AND FAMILY
(Mary Kane Russell White, Mary Peltz Russell, Katherine Hun Peltz, Caroline Gale Hun, Elizabeth Wells
  Gale, Elizabeth McDonald Wells, Richard McDonald, Maj. Richard, Col. William, William MacDonel)

Leslie White-Siek (b. 1973) is the third daughter of Richard Booth and Mary Kane (Russell) White. In 1990, she was part of a group of volunteer youth from the U.S., Russia and the Ukraine to rehearse and perform a musical play called "Peace Child." The idea of the play was to promote peace between the U.S., Russia and the Ukraine "in order to effectively address and resolve common problems concerning the post- 'Cold War' world."[390] The play dealt with shared social and environmental concerns such as deforestation, air and water pollution, child welfare, poverty, racial and gender inequality, religious intolerance, and nuclear arms issues.

Leslie continued to pursue her passion for the theatre. She attended New York University and received a B.F.A. in acting in 1995, and then went on to a successful career in show business in both New York and Los Angeles as part of the Emmy Award-winning cast of the TV series *Law and Order*, playing the role of Laura Abbot in the "Tabloid" episode written by David Black and Alec Baldwin. She also performed with The Nada Faust Festival and The Lincoln Center Theater Festival and appeared in a number of commercial spots including AT&T, Applebee's and Citibank.

In 2004, Leslie received a master's degree in landscape architecture from the University of Pennsylvania. She is married to Michael Rolf Siek of Aegis Capital Ventures. They have a son, Tristram Michael Siek, born Apr. 8, 2006.[391]

Nowadays, Leslie is the owner, designer and lead consultant for Leslie White-Siek Designs in Fairfield County, Connecticut. She works with the Norwalk Tree Alliance to inspire school children to appreciate the importance of trees in their community. She also works with Norwalk School Farm 2 Table to install vegetable gardens at schools to help children learn the importance of food and diet.

Leslie has a variety of interests and concerns including not only arts and culture, but also animal welfare, civil rights, human rights, social services and the environment.[392]

> "I have really enjoyed being a stay at home mom the most of all my pursuits," says Leslie. "It is the toughest and most rewarding by far!!"[393]

KATHERINE RUSSELL SCHMIDT (1943-2008) AND FAMILY
(Mary Peltz Russell, Katherine Hun Peltz, Caroline Gale Hun, Elizabeth Wells Gale, Elizabeth McDonald Wells, Richard McDonald, Maj. Richard, Col. William, William MacDonel)

Katherine Russell was the second of three daughters born to Dr. Theodore Burg and Mary (Peltz) Russell. Born in 1943,[394] she married Benno C. Schmidt Jr. (born Mar. 20, 1942), who was Dean of the Columbia Law School from 1984-1986, and the 20th president of Yale University from 1986-1992. Later, he served as president and chief executive of the Edison Project (now EdisonLearning), a New York company that privately operates public schools. Benno also made appearances in two Woody Allen films, *Husbands and Wives* (1992), and *Hannah and Her Sisters* (1986), in which he played Dr. Smith, the first husband of Mia Farrow's character.[395]

Benno's father, Benno C. Schmidt Sr., was a senior partner of J. H. Whitney & Company, the first venture capital firm in the United States.[396]

Katherine Russell Schmidt was a volunteer teacher in the early childhood program of the Colorado Springs Head Start program in Colorado Springs, El Paso County, Colorado.[397] She passed away in 2008 at the age of 65.[398]

Katherine and Benno C. Schmidt Jr. had two children: Elizabeth Hun Schmidt and Benno Schmidt III.[399]

ELIZABETH HUN SCHMIDT LIFTIN (Living)
(Katherine Russell Schmidt, Mary Peltz Russell, Katherine Hun Peltz, Caroline Gale Hun, Elizabeth Wells
 Gale, Elizabeth McDonald Wells, Richard McDonald, Maj. Richard, Col. William, William MacDonel)

Elizabeth Hun Schmidt is the daughter of Benno Jr. and Katherine (Russell) Schmidt. She married Eric Liftin, the son of John M. and Leni Liftin, on Oct. 5, 1996. Elizabeth graduated from Wesleyan University in 1989 and earned a Ph.D. in literature from New York University in 2003.[400] Her husband, Eric, graduated from Yale and received his master's degree in architecture from Columbia University. He designed websites for Firefly Network, taught at Columbia University, and now owns MESH Architectures, designing buildings and beautiful environments. He is also the founder and CEO of Tunnel X, a platform for secure, private conversation.[401]

Elizabeth Hun Schmidt is the chief curriculum officer for Ascend Learning Charter Schools. Formerly, she taught courses in literature at Sarah Lawrence College and Barnard College and worked as poetry editor for the *New York Times Book Review* and assistant editor for *The New Yorker*.[402] She edited *Poems of New York* (2002)[403] and *The Poets Laureate Anthology* (2010) with poet Billy Collins.[404]

Elizabeth's many interests include animal welfare, arts and culture, civil rights and social action, and science and technology.[405] She is the mother of two collegiate artists.[406]

PHOEBE RUSSELL MACADAMS OZUNA (1947-Living) AND FAMILY
(Mary Peltz Russell, Katherine Hun Peltz, Caroline Gale Hun, Elizabeth Wells Gale, Elizabeth McDonald
 Wells, Richard McDonald, Maj. Richard, Col. William, William MacDonel)

Phoebe Russell, the youngest of three daughters born to Dr. Theodore Burg and Mary (Peltz) Russell, was born on Nov. 14, 1947 and raised in New York City, and Princeton, New Jersey.[407] She later moved to California where she has spent most of her adult life.

Phoebe married, firstly, Lewis Perry MacAdams Jr., the son of Lewis Perry and Marjorie Lee (Rosenthal) MacAdams, who was born in San Angelo, Tom Green County, Texas, on Oct. 12, 1944. Lewis graduated from Princeton University in 1966, then received his master's from the State University of New York (SUNY) at Buffalo in 1968.[408] He is a prominent poet who was part of New York City's avant-garde poetry scene of the 1960's and 1970's. He moved to the village of Bolinas, an experimental community in Marin County, on the coast of California.[409]

From 1975-1978, Lewis was director of the Poetry Center at San Francisco State University. His published poetry collections include, among others, *Water Charms* (1968), *The Poetry Room* (1971), *News from Niman Farm* (1976), *Blind Date* (1981), *Africa and the Marriage of Walt Whitman and Marilyn Monroe* (1982), *The River: Books One Two and Three (2007)*, and *Dear Oxygen* (2011). He also produced and directed the 1986 documentary *What Happened to Kerouac?*[410] as well as a recent CD *Good Grief* (2015).

Lewis is the co-founder and president of Friends of the Los Angeles River (FOLAR) a non-profit organization started in 1986, whose mission is to protect and restore the natural and historic heritage of the Los Angeles River and its riparian habitat through inclusive planning, education and wise stewardship.[411]

Lewis and Phoebe (Russell) MacAdams have two sons:
1. Ocean Lee (b. 1971, m. Suzanne Petren-Moritz)
2. William Blaze (b. 1973, m. Mikiko Suzuki, now separated)

Lewis and Phoebe's marriage ended in divorce.

Phoebe is also an accomplished poet. She taught English and creative writing at Roosevelt High School in Los Angeles for 26 years, retiring in 2011.[412]

Known as Phoebe MacAdams in the poetry world, she is a founding member of both the Los Angeles Poetry Festival and Cahuenga Press, which has published 23 books since it was founded in 1989.[413] She has published six books of poetry: *Sunday* (1983), *Ever* (1985), *Ordinary Snake Dance* (1994), *Livelihood* (2003), *Strange Grace* (2007) and *Touching Stone* (2012).[414]

For two years, Phoebe coordinated the Gasoline Alley reading series on Melrose Avenue with fellow poet, Bill Mohr.[415] She shared some thoughts about her work as both a poet and teacher that Bill featured on his website:

> "Very few poets make enough money from their poems to live. It is rare. Most poets teach. Teaching English or literature allows you to think about writing all day. It also gives you time to write. Even in high school teaching, there are long breaks – Christmas, spring and summer – which are times that you can spend writing... Poetry is a tracking of spirit: keeping track of spirit through the breath and through words. It is a very important job, but it is not a skill that is really marketable. Adding the market, selling spirit – how to do that? It would ruin it, no? Perhaps it is a good thing that poets can't market themselves strictly as poets. It is important to keep this activity separate, to keep it in a sacred space. However, one has to figure out how to have a decent life while maintaining that space – not an easy task. I decided I wanted to do something that mattered to me, that I thought was an important job, and that provided enough money for me to live a relatively comfortable life. Teaching fulfilled all these criteria."[416]

Phoebe now lives with her second husband, Ron Ozuna, in Pasadena, Los Angeles County, California.[417] Ron was an award-winning science teacher at Roosevelt High School. He is now an accomplished bird photographer. He also retired from teaching in 2011.[418]

OCEAN LEE MACADAMS (1971-Living) AND FAMILY
(Phoebe Russell MacAdams, Mary Peltz Russell, Katherine Hun Peltz, Caroline Gale Hun, Elizabeth Wells Gale, Elizabeth McDonald Wells, Richard McDonald, Maj. Richard, Col. William, William MacDonel)

Ocean Lee MacAdams is the eldest son of poets Lewis Perry Jr. and Phoebe (Russell) MacAdams. He was born on Mar. 30, 1971, in San Francisco County, California.[419]

Ocean is currently senior vice president, programming and acquisitions, for the Madison Square Garden Company.[420] Formerly, Ocean worked as general manager of Warner Music Group, as senior vice president of programming for Current TV, and as senior vice president of MTV Networks. He is a 1994 graduate of Columbia University in New York City, and now lives in Brooklyn.[421]

Ocean married Suzanne Petren-Moritz, who graduated with a B.A. in fine arts and philosophy from Harvard University in 1993 and then received her M.B.A. from Harvard Business School in 2001. She is now CEO at Market News International.[422] They have two daughters, Astrid and Lena, as well as one son, Axel.[423]

WILLIAM BLAZE MACADAMS (1973-Living)
(Phoebe Russell MacAdams, Mary Peltz Russell, Katherine Hun Peltz, Caroline Gale Hun, Elizabeth Wells
  Gale, Elizabeth McDonald Wells, Richard McDonald, Maj. Richard, Col. William, William MacDonel)

William Blaze "Will" MacAdams is the second son of poets Lewis Perry Jr. and Phoebe (Russell) MacAdams. He was born on July 14, 1973, in San Francisco County, California.[424] Will attended the Harvard School in North Hollywood, Los Angeles County, California,[425] then received his B.A. in Theater Studies from Yale University in 1994, and an M.F.A. in Theater Directing from Columbia University, in 2006.[426]

Will married Mikiko Suzuki. Both Will and Mikiko are accomplished theatre artists.

Will creates theatre projects, writes original plays and directs. A few of his projects are *The Black Dirt Cycle*, a cycle of three plays about immigration and soil; *Eye to Eye*, a play about racism and youth-police relations; and *Cruising the Divide*, a play about race, class, and the celebration of the Kentucky Derby. He has directed productions for Actors Theatre of Louisville, Humana Festival, Barnard College and Columbia University. He was awarded the Rockefeller Foundation's Next Generation Leadership Fellowship as well as a Yale University Bates Fellowship, which took him to Indonesia to learn Javanese Shadow Puppetry.[427]

From 2012-2015, Will taught acting, directing and theatre for social change as visiting assistant professor of theatre at Hampshire College in Amherst, Hampshire County, Massachusetts.

Will's wife, Mikiko Suzuki MacAdams, from whom he is now separated, is a theatre set designer and a member of United Scenic Artist Local USA-829. She has designed sets for companies across the U.S. and internationally including Oregon Shakespeare Festival; Nikikai Opera of Tokyo, Japan; Biwako Hall, Otsu, Japan; Seattle Repertory Theatre; Long Wharf Theatre; The Ensemble Studio Theatre (Off-Broadway); Yale Opera; Yale School of Drama; Actors Theatre of Louisville; New Jersey Opera Theatre; Cincinnati Playhouse; and Columbia University. She was also associate scenic designer on several Broadway productions including *Awake and Sing* (2006), *Cymbeline* (2007), *South Pacific* (2008), *Jo Turner's Come and Gone* (2009), *That Championship Season* (2011), *Golden Boy* (2012), and *The Bridges of Madison County* (2014).

Mikiko also has taught set design courses for Fordham University in New York City, the Mason Gross School of the Arts at Rutgers University in New Brunswick, New Jersey, and Hampshire College, in Amherst, Massachusetts.[428]

PHILIP PELTZ (1915-2001) AND FAMILY
(Katherine Hun Peltz, Caroline Gale Hun, Elizabeth Wells Gale, Elizabeth McDonald Wells,
 Richard McDonald, Maj. Richard, Col. William, William MacDonel)

Philip "Peter" Peltz, the fourth and youngest child of William Law Learned and Katherine (Hun) Peltz, was born on Dec. 18, 1915, in Albany, Albany County, New York.[429] He attended Yale University (Class of 1938) and was a member of the famous singing group, The Whiffenpoofs. They sang a number of old standards including "When You Wore a Tulip," "Hand Me Down My Walking Cane," "The Whiffenpoof Song," and "I Had a Dream Dear."[430] Philip also earned a master's degree in history from Yale.[431]

During World War II, Philip served as a lieutenant in the U.S. Navy in the Mediterranean and the Pacific.[432]

Philip was an artist, a self-employed wood carver.[433] He was best known for his hand-carved and painted birds, which he sold for more than 40 years from his unique residence called "The Bird Barn" in Sandwich, Barnstable County, Massachusetts.[434] His carvings became so popular that even Jackie Kennedy, the wife of President John F. Kennedy, was "known to have owned at least three of his birds."[435]

On Aug. 9, 1941, in Hartford, Hartford County, Connecticut, Philip married Elizabeth Davenport "Betsy" Hooper, the daughter of William Thomas and Florence Davenport (Wright) Hooper. Betsy was born Dec. 19, 1919, in Hartford and attended Pine Manor College in Chestnut Hill, a suburb of Boston, Massachusetts. She joined the Women's Army Corps (WACs) during World War II and served as a driver in San Francisco to greet servicemen returning home from the Pacific front.[436]

Philip and Betsy had one son, Peter, and one daughter, Sarah, better known as Shawnee. The family lived in Sandwich, Barnstable County, Massachusetts, where Elizabeth was an active volunteer in community affairs. She made jellies and preserves from the fruits of her garden and was a master at flower arrangement.[437]

In 1968, they moved to Bonita Springs, Lee County, Florida, where Philip continued to carve. He also liked to hunt and fish and had a terrific sense of humor.[438]

Betsy passed away on Feb. 29, 2000 (leap year) in Naples Hospital in Florida, at the age of 80. She loved family and friends and had a great sense of humor.[439] Philip died a little over a year later in Morrisville, Lamoille County, Vermont, on Mar. 20, 2001, at the age of 85.[440]

REP. PETER PELTZ (1946-Living) AND FAMILY
(Philip Peltz, Katherine Hun Peltz, Caroline Gale Hun, Elizabeth Wells Gale, Elizabeth McDonald Wells,
 Richard McDonald, Maj. Richard, Col. William, William MacDonel)

Peter Peltz, the eldest child of Philip and Elizabeth (Hooper) Peltz, was born on Apr. 21, 1946, in Albany, Albany County, New York.[441] He received a B.F.A. from Tufts University in 1971.

Peter married Catherine "Cacky" Gantt, the daughter of Benjamin Jr. and Doris (Henrich) Gantt.[442] Peter's father-in-law, Benjamin Gantt Jr., was an attorney in Seattle, Washington, and a United States Marine Corps veteran of World War II, who took part in the landing on Iwo Jima and later served on Guam.[443]

Peter and Cacky live in Woodbury, Washington County, Vermont. Cacky has worked in art education for more than 25 years. She attended the University of California at Berkeley, graduating in 1969 with a B.F.A in printmaking and painting. She has worked for the Boston Museum of Fine Arts, as well as Stowe Elementary School for 18 years as an art teacher. She received a grant to conduct a Child to Child Art Exchange between students in Stowe and Kenya, Africa, as part of an effort to promote good will and understanding among young people of different cultures.[444] Recently, she has served on the Committee of Practitioners for the Vermont Agency of Education[445] and as vice-chair of the Woodbury Town School Board.[446]

Peter is the owner of Peter Peltz Construction, Inc.[447] A Democrat, he served in the Vermont State House of Representatives from 2006-2014.[448]

Peter and Cacky have two children:
1. Aysha (m. Todd Whitney Wahlstrom)
2. Alex (m. Ann Koivunen)

AYSHA PELTZ (Living) AND FAMILY
(Peter Peltz, Philip Peltz, Katherine Hun Peltz, Caroline Gale Hun, Elizabeth Wells Gale, Elizabeth
  McDonald Wells, Richard McDonald, Maj. Richard, Col. William, William MacDonel)

Aysha Peltz, the eldest child of Peter and Cacky Peltz, is a ceramic artist specializing in pottery. She received her B.F.A. and M.F.A. from the School of Art and Design at New York State College of Ceramics at Alfred University, Alfred, New York.

Aysha teaches, lectures and exhibits her works both nationally and internationally.[449] In 2005, she won the Emerging Artist Award at the National Council for the Education of the Ceramic Arts. She has taught at the Arrowmont School of Arts and Crafts in Gatlinburg, Tennessee, and the Kansas City Arts Institute. She is currently on the Visual Arts Faculty at Bennington College in Vermont.[450]

Aysha says of her work, "I alter freshly thrown forms to achieve the look of an action that has just occurred, a moment frozen in time. I think of my pots as imagined space and through them I build landscape and terrain."[451]

Aysha now lives in Whitingham, Windham County, Vermont. She and her husband, Todd Whitney Wahlstrom, also a ceramic artist, work out of their studios at Town Hill Pottery in Whitingham. They have two children: Ellis and Maeve.[452]

ALEX PELTZ (Living)
(Peter Peltz, Philip Peltz, Katherine Hun Peltz, Caroline Gale Hun, Elizabeth Wells Gale, Elizabeth
  McDonald Wells, Richard McDonald, Maj. Richard, Col. William, William MacDonel)

Alex Peltz, the second child of Peter and Cacky Peltz, studied art and anthropology at Hamilton College in Clinton, Oneida County, New York. He and his wife, Ann Koivunen, operate Peltz Creative, "a Philadelphia-based cultural advisory and implementation studio that provides art, design, and communication solutions."[453]

Ann earned a B.F.A. in Graphic Design and a B.A. in Spanish Language & Culture at the University of Michigan in Ann Arbor. She worked for The Center for Emerging Visual Artists to serve as director of the Philadelphia Open Studio Tours. She has developed an expertise for envisioning, mounting, and managing visual art exhibitions. She is a member of the boards of the 40th Street Artists-In-Residence Program and The Reiki School & Clinic.[454]

Alex co-founded Posters for the People, an initiative to archive and celebrate posters that were created during the Works Progress Administration (WPA). He is a member of the Philadelphia chapter of the American Institute of Graphic Arts (AIGA).[455]

SARAH DAVENPORT "SHAWNEE" PELTZ UNGER (1949-Living) AND FAMILY
(Philip Peltz, Katherine Hun Peltz, Caroline Gale Hun, Elizabeth Wells Gale, Elizabeth McDonald Wells, Richard McDonald, Maj. Richard, Col. William, William MacDonel)

Sarah Davenport "Shawnee" Peltz, the younger of two children of Philip and Elizabeth (Hooper) Peltz, was born on Mar. 1, 1949, in Albany, Albany County, New York. When she was three years old, her family moved to Sandwich, Massachusetts. She recalls having a pleasant childhood, seeing friends, riding bikes, going to the beach and walking on the boardwalk. She and her family enjoyed taking a boat out for a day of fishing, clamming and picnicking on Cape Cod.[456]

Shawnee was quite athletic from an early age. She loved to play kick the can, baseball and especially, tennis. She learned to play tennis on a clay court in Sandwich and still plays with the USTA to this day.

After graduating from high school, Shawnee went to Boston University where she met her future husband, Philip Axon Unger, a senior at Harvard. In 1969-1970, she and Philip, along with their dog Sasha, spent a year traveling across the U.S. and Canada in a milk truck they dubbed "Wilbur." They took mostly back roads as Wilbur's top speed was about 40 mph. The highlight of the trip was spending 3 months on Keno Lake in British Columbia. They hunted, fished, trapped and lived off the land in a very remote area they accessed with an inflatable boat. The only human being they saw the whole time was one lone fisherman.

On June 10, 1972, Philip and Shawnee were married in Sandwich. They honeymooned in Bangkok, Thailand. Phil's parents, Leonard and Anne (Axon) Unger, were living there at the time. Leonard was serving as U.S. Ambassador to Thailand. Phil's siblings flew in from the U.S. and the entire Unger family had a wonderful reunion of sorts.

Phil and Shawnee spent the next 9 months traveling through Thailand, Indonesia, India, Malaysia and Nepal.[457] When they returned to the United States, Phil, having obtained a biology degree from Harvard, was offered a job as a technician with the Smithsonian to be a host and guide for visiting scientists in Laos. So in 1974 and 1975, Shawnee and Phil lived in a village called Ban Thalat in Laos with no plumbing or electricity.[458]

In 1975, the Pathet Lao, a communist political organization, took over the country. Phil, Shawnee and their three-month-old daughter, Tess, were evacuated to Bangkok. The Pathet Lao were closely associated with the Vietnamese communists and fought against the anti-communist forces in the Vietnam War.

Philip and Shawnee have two children:

1. Tess (b. Jan. 5, 1975, Bangkok, Thailand)
2. Katherine Elizabeth "Kate" (b. Aug. 14, 1981, Boulder, CO)

From 1975-1985, the family lived in Boulder, Boulder County, Colorado. Shawnee graduated from the University of Colorado at Boulder with a teaching degree, while Phil received a Ph.D. from that same institution in limnology (the study of inland waters). Later, they lived in Baldwinsville, New York; Lusby, Maryland; and Austin, Texas. In 1992, they moved to Auburn, Placer County, California.[459]

Shawnee is a public school teacher who works part time with tribal (Indian) students. She and Philip divorced in 2008.

Daughter Tess is a single mom. She obtained her master's degree from Mill's College, works as a teacher, and lives in Oakland, California, with her son, Gabriel Garza.

Daughter Kate is an artist and art teacher. She graduated from the Pacific Northwest College of Art in Portland, Oregon, and now lives with her partner, Luke Geniella-, in Los Angeles.[460]

The Ungers made a return trip to Laos about 25 years after they left. Phil and Shawnee showed their daughters the village of Ban Thalat and the house in which they lived. The whole experience was, as Shawnee recalled, a "great, soulful trip."[461]

———⊂※⊃———

CATHERINE J. WELLS GALE (1829-1922)
(Elizabeth McDonald Wells, Richard McDonald, Maj. Richard, Col. William, William MacDonel)

Catherine J. Wells,[462] the second child of Philander and Elizabeth (McDonald) Wells, was born Feb. 14, 1829, in Troy, Rensselaer County, New York.[463] She lived with her parents at least until 1870, when she was about 41 years old.

Catherine's elder sister, Elizabeth Van Schoonhovan Wells, married John Benjamin Gale, an attorney, about 1846. When Elizabeth died about 1871, Catherine married her sister's widowed husband, John Gale, in 1872. He died in 1906 in Williamstown, Berkshire County, Massachusetts, at the age of 82.

Catherine lived quite a bit longer – to the age of 93. She died in Williamstown on Dec. 6, 1922, and was buried in Oakwood Cemetery in Troy.[464]

Chapter 5

PROVING THE LINEAGE:
How DNA Can Confirm the Ancestry of
Richard McDonald of Lansingburgh

As we were researching and writing this book, it became clear that it would be extremely helpful if a living male McDonald descendant of Richard McDonald of Lansingburgh would have his Y-DNA tested, but to date there are only a few known male McDonalds of Richard's line still alive. They are descendants of Richard Earl MacDonald Sr. (1894-1980) of Albany County, New York. All of the other known McDonald descendant lines of Richard have died out.

We strongly urge at least one of those male descendants of Richard Earl MacDonald Sr. to take the Y-DNA test.

WHY IS THIS SO IMPORTANT?

As the foremost authority on the McDonalds of Somerset County, having done extensive research on the various McDonald families in that place and time, this author can state that the research presented in this book clearly demonstrates to his satisfaction that Richard of Lansingburgh is indeed the son of Maj. Richard McDonald of New Jersey.

However, the documentary evidence is sparse. We have cemetery records stating Richard of Lansingburgh was the son of Richard and Catharine McDonald of New Jersey, and we have court records showing George McDonald, son of Maj. Richard, was the guardian of Lansing McDonald, son of Richard of Lansingburgh. Thankfully these records have survived. Otherwise, we would never know that Richard of Lansingburgh was the son of Maj. Richard.

There is plenty of circumstantial evidence as well to support Richard of Lansingburgh as son of Maj. Richard, particularly the fact that Maj. Richard identified his son Richard in his will in 1820. The will tells us the son was already deceased, but he did have issue. Richard of Lansingburgh, we now know, died in 1812, before Maj. Richard made his will. It makes perfect sense that he would move to New York, not too far from his elder brother, William R. McDonald, whose identity was also recently discovered – and proven through DNA tests.[465]

There will, however, always be skeptics who have their doubts about Richard of Lansingburgh being Maj. Richard McDonald's son. That is all well and good. It is always wise to keep an open mind, especially as new evidence emerges.

The problem is that absolute proof is very hard to come by in genealogy. There is an opportunity for human error in every step of the record-keeping process. It is also not unusual for people to completely "make up" stories about their family lineage or jump to conclusions about their ancestry with insufficient evidence and research. Then there is always the possibility that somewhere along the line going back in time, someone who was believed to be the son or daughter of a certain father or mother may, in fact, not have been that parent's legitimate child. That child may have been adopted or born out of wedlock to an unknown partner. We all know about family secrets. The farther you go back in time, the more questionable the genetic relationships from parents to children become, because there simply is no way of knowing for sure.

That's why taking a Y-DNA test is so important, so that future generations can have the highest level of certainty that their ancestor Richard McDonald of Lansingburgh is indeed the son of Maj. Richard McDonald. After all, it may not be long before all the male MacDonald descendants of Maj. Richard McDonald have died out. At that point, it will be impossible to "prove" the lineage.

HOW DOES THE Y-DNA TEST WORK?

The Y-chromosome is handed down from father to son going all the way back in time, but it is only handed down to males. Maj. Richard McDonald handed down the Y-DNA of his forebears to his sons, including Richard of Lansingburgh. They, in turn, handed it down to their sons.

So far, we have two descendants of Maj. Richard McDonald who have taken the Y-DNA test. The first, Michael John McDonald, is descended from Maj. Richard's son, George McDonald, the lawyer. The second, Thomas Corey McDonald, is descended from Maj. Richard's eldest son, William R. McDonald. The Y-DNA of Michael John and Thomas Corey matches.[466] That tells us that they are indeed both descended from Maj. Richard.

If one of the male descendants of Richard Earl MacDonald Sr. (1894-1980) takes the test and it matches the Y-DNA of Michael John and Thomas Corey, then we will know beyond any reasonable doubt that Richard of Lansingburgh is truly the son of Maj. Richard McDonald of Somerset County, New Jersey

So you see, whoever takes the test will be doing a great favor for ALL the descendants of Richard McDonald of Lansingburgh and indeed the entire extended family of Maj. Richard McDonald, whose lineage and legacy have been lost to so many for almost 200 years.

HOW TO TAKE THE TEST

The test is very easy to take. You just get a DNA kit from a testing company, swab your cheek, place the swab into the package provided and send it off to the company. We highly recommend that you test with FamilyTreeDNA familytreedna.com. Besides having an excellent reputation, they also have access to the results of Michael John and Thomas Corey so that we can quickly determine if they match the new samples.

It is also very important to test for at least 67 markers. Anything less will not be helpful.

IMPLICATIONS FOR THE ENTIRE MCDONALD CLAN

Thanks to the DNA tests of Michael John and Thomas Corey, we now have a benchmark for identifying other lines of McDonalds who may be descended from Maj. Richard McDonald and his ancestors.

It is exciting to consider that there may be other unknown lines of McDonald descendants of Richard McDonald of Lansingburgh living today. Remember, for example, we don't know what happened to Richard's son, Jacob McDonald, who reportedly lived in Georgia.

There may also be many more lines of American McDonalds, MacDonalds, MacDonnells, McDaniels, etc. who are descended from Maj. Richard McDonald's immigrant Scottish ancestor, who have not yet been positively identified. If we can determine that immigrant's identity through DNA testing and paper trails, we may finally discover where he came from in Scotland.

We strongly urge all male McDonalds (no matter how you spell it) to take a Y-DNA test for at least 67 markers. All test takers should join the Clan Donald USA Genetic Genealogy Project (it's free). They can help you to compare and analyze the results, especially when it comes to identifying the ancient forebears in Scotland.

In fact, we urge McDonald males from all over the world to take the Y-DNA test. The more who test, the more all of us will be able to learn about the lineages and the histories of the various branches in the entire MacDonald Clan.

Chapter 6

EXCITING NEW REVELATIONS IN MCDONALD FAMILY HISTORY

THE SEARCH FOR LOST BRANCHES OF THE MCDONALD FAMILY TREE

Since *A Revolutionary American Family: The McDonalds of Somerset County, New Jersey* was published in 2015, the research on the McDonald family has been ongoing. Two new lines of McDonalds were discovered: the line of William R. McDonald and Abigail Fowler, published separately, and the line of Richard and Catharine (Lansing) McDonald of Lansingburgh, New York, described in this book. William R. and Richard were both sons of Maj. Richard McDonald (1734-1820) of Pluckemin, New Jersey. Their stories and the stories of their descendants shed further light on the extraordinary history of this McDonald family.

There was also a George C. (or G.) MacDonald, an oysterman and painter, born in New Jersey about 1803-1806, married Jane Smith in 1823 in Bergen, Hudson County, New Jersey, and died Nov. 30, 1877, in North Plainfield, Somerset County, New Jersey, who was thought to be the mysterious George, son of Col. George McDonald (1768-1820), the lawyer, who was also a son of Maj. Richard McDonald. A descendant of this George C. MacDonald, one Arthur R. McDonald, took a Y-DNA test. The results showed that he was not from the same McDonald ancestral line as Maj. Richard McDonald. He belonged to a completely different haplogroup (I-P37). It is now speculated that he might have been a descendant of Thomas MacDonald, who settled in Hudson County, New Jersey, about 1776, and has no known relation to the McDonalds of Somerset County, New Jersey.

IS LADY MARY PEMBERTON THE MOTHER OF MAJ. RICHARD MCDONALD?

Now that more people are discovering their McDonald roots, more interesting tales of family history are coming to the fore. The most exciting revelation revolves around a mysterious Lady Mary Pemberton. Could she be the mother of Maj. Richard McDonald, the first wife of Col. William McDonald (d. 1799)?

Despite the extensive research that went into *A Revolutionary American Family,* the first wife of Col. William McDonald was never discovered. Yet Col. William and his McDonald family were in the upper echelons of colonial American society. Col. William was the High Sheriff of Somerset County, appointed by New Jersey Governor William Franklin, the son of Founding Father Benjamin Franklin. Evidence strongly suggests that Col. William was the son of a yeoman William MacDonel and his wife Florance. It has always been a tantalizing mystery as to how Col. William McDonald received an education and rose to such prominence.

Col. William's son, Maj. Richard McDonald, was a man of wealth and status. It is believed he worked directly with Gen. George Washington in the Revolutionary War. Was his unknown mother a woman of high society?

In 2016, Peter Macdonald Blachly a descendant of Mayor Richard McDonald (1803-1894), who was a grandson of Maj. Richard McDonald, sent the following note:

> This morning I happened across a postcard from 1945 addressed to Mrs. William A. Howell (aka Katherine Macdonald Howell, daughter of George E Macdonald), my great grandmother on my maternal grandmother's side. On the back side it has an obituary—apparently from 1923—for Mary Macdonald DeWitt. The obit has one paragraph about Mary, then goes on to praise Mary's great-great grandmother, Lady Mary Pemberton, who "gave up title and wealth for love against her family's wishes to come to America…"—or something to that effect.[467]

Mary MacDonald DeWitt's full name was Mary Antoinette MacDonald. She lived from 1844-1923. She was a great granddaughter of Maj. Richard McDonald. Her great great grandmother would have been Maj. Richard's mother, the first wife of Col. William McDonald. Furthermore, the other great great grandmothers in Mary DeWitt's ancestry have been identified and none of them is a Pemberton.

Mary MacDonald DeWitt's great great grandmothers are:
1. Unknown first wife of Col. William McDonald
2. Kniertje Montfoort Schamp
3. Aeltje Olden DeGroot
4. Sarah Compton Castner
5. Agnes Jones Eastburn
6. Elizabeth Loofbourrow Inglis
7. Unknown White
8. Unknown Kennedy

The Whites and Kennedys shown above are unknown, but their children immigrated from Dublin, Ireland, so it is very unlikely they are the Lady Mary Pemberton in question. Agnes Jones Eastburn also seems unlikely to be Lady Pemberton.

Following Peter Macdonald Blachy's initial inquiry, he kindly sent the entire death notice of Mary MacDonald DeWitt, transcribed below:

> With the entrance into eternal rest of Mary Antoinette Macdonald, wife of the late David Miller deWitt, there passed one of the gentlewomen of the old school. With her tender sympathy for the joys and sorrows of all with whom she came in contact, only those to whom she gave it so unsparingly, can measure the void that is left.
>
> Her wonderful personal beauty was a fitting casket to enshrine the jewel of her soul. When her great, great grandmother, Lady Mary Pemberton, for whom Mrs. deWitt was named, following the dictates of her heart, gave up title and wealth in opposition to her family and came with her husband to America, it was to found a large family, conspicuous for its piety, loyal Americanism

and the unsullied faithfulness of its members to their country's welfare which they were often called to administer.

Devoted and unselfish in all the relations of life, as daughter, wife, mother and friend the sense of Mrs. deWitt's loss will only be deepened by the passing of time. J.H.B.[468]

The mystery of the origins of the family of Col. William McDonald deepen considerably with this new revelation. Was Lady Pemberton, in fact, the mother of Maj. Richard McDonald? We cannot say for sure, but it does seem to be a very good possibility. Did Col. William McDonald and Lady Mary Pemberton come to America as man and wife, she "giving up title and wealth in opposition to her family?" If true, it might explain why Col. William and his McDonald family were of such high social status.

Unfortunately, subsequent research has failed to uncover any further information about Lady Mary Pemberton. It may be possible that she was a granddaughter or other relation of Sir Francis Pemberton (1624-1697), Lord Chief Justice of the King's Bench whose descendants are the Pembertons of Trumpington Hall, high sheriffs of Cambridge. If so, that might help explain why Col. William McDonald became Justice of the Quorum and High Sheriff of Somerset County, New Jersey. He certainly must have had connections to very prominent and influential people. Although it is thought that Col. William was probably born in America, could it be that somehow he went to school in England, perhaps Cambridge? Could it be he met Lady Pemberton there, courted her and brought her to America against the wishes of her family? It's just a theory, nothing more. More evidence is definitely needed to unravel the mystery.

MARGARET COE WAS THE SECOND WIFE OF COL. WILLIAM MCDONALD

Another previously undiscovered document came to our attention regarding the surname of Col. McDonald's second wife, Margaret (1733-1808):

New Jersey, Deaths and Burials Index, 1798-1971

Name:	Margaret McDonald [Margaret Coe]
Birth Date:	abt 1733
Death Date:	2 Aug 1808
Cemetery Name:	Old Presbyterian Graveyard
Death Age:	75 years
Gender:	Female
Father Name:	William Coe
Comments:	Old Presby. Graveyard, Hamilton & East Sts.
FHL Film Number:	543520

We can now state with confidence that Col. William McDonald's second wife was Margaret Coe, the daughter of William Coe.

DNA POINTS TO FERMANAGH, IRELAND, AS THE EARLY HOMELAND OF OUR MCDONALDS

The Clan Colla 425 Null Project referenced in *A Revolutionary American Family*, p. 329, is still studying the DNA of closely related branches of McDonalds (and other surnames), including the McDonalds of Somerset County.

The DNA evidence, at this point, suggests that the ancestors of the McDonalds of Somerset County were in ancient times from the Fermanaugh and Monaghan districts of Ireland. Clan Donald believes this Irish DNA branch left the Fermanagh Valley to join Somerled and his father to fight the Vikings in Morvern, Scotland. Consequently, these Irishmen remained in Scotland and merged with Clan Donald to become clansmen sometime about the year 1100 A.D.

Researcher Shawn Marchinek speculates that our McDonalds may have been part of the Macdonalds of Ardnamurchan, which is located north of Morvern.

> The Macdonalds (or MacIains) of Ardnamurchan were one of the first Clans to become Protestant. Then the Campbells broke their clan and scattered them in the early 1600's. The Ardnamurchans became pirates for a while and ended up settling mostly in Morvern and some into Badenoch. No none Ardnamurchan Macdonalds have been located or tested for DNA. So I have a theory that with so many null 425 Macdonalds/Macdaniels our ancestors could have been Ardnamurchan Macdonalds.[469]

Marchinek also reported in April 2019 that a related DNA branch of McDonalds, who are participating in the study, now believe their ancestor John Sparks McDonald was the grandson of Angus McDonald (b. 1769 on the Isle of Skye; d. 1861, NC), who lies buried in Douglas Cemetery, Laurinburg, Scotland County, North Carolina.[470] Marchinek speculates that the common ancestor which binds many of our related DNA branches together could be the 1st to 3rd great grandfather of Angus McDonald, c. 1500. If so, then it may be that the McDonalds of Somerset County were somehow part of Clan Sleat on the Isle of Skye.

None of this is provable at this time, of course, but we have some good theories to pursue.

Genealogy is an endlessly fascinating enterprise. As time goes by, more revelations will be forthcoming and we will learn even more about this intriguing and astonishing McDonald family of Somerset County, New Jersey.

AFTERWORD

The descendants of Richard and Catharine (Lansing) McDonald have certainly made their mark on American history across locales in every region of the United States. They represent, however, just one branch of the much larger McDonald Family Tree, whose progenitors were Col. William McDonald and Maj. Richard McDonald of Pluckemin, New Jersey. They were there when America was being born and helped to shape its destiny. The circumstances of their lives are worthy of a Hollywood movie, complete with envy, lust, murder – and dinner with George Washington! And it's all true.

In fact, the fascinating story of the McDonald forefathers goes all the way back to 17th century Scotland, a dark period known to history as "The Killing Time," and is told in its entirety in *A Revolutionary American Family: The McDonalds of Somerset County, New Jersey* (Indelible Mark Publishing, May 2015).

Indeed, if the line of Richard and Catharine (Lansing) McDonald had come to light a few months earlier, this present manuscript would have been incorporated into its pages. This descendant line certainly deserves to take its place there among the other descendants of Maj. Richard McDonald.

In 2015, this book was produced as an e-book. Now in 2021, it is a physical, soft cover book that you can hold in your hands, put on your bookshelf, and easily hand down to your descendants. The same goes for another newly discovered branch of the tree, available previously as an e-book, now in soft cover, *William R. McDonald and Abigail Fowler of Herkimer County, New York and Their Descendants*. William R. McDonald of Herkimer County was an older brother of Richard McDonald.

Genealogy is always in process as new material comes to light. The research on the entire McDonald family will continue. No doubt in the future more will be revealed and some of the mysteries will be explained.

We invite you to become a part of this research and to contribute what you have to share about your branch of the tree.

Also be sure to check out our Facebook page, *The McDonalds of Somerset County, NJ, Descendants*, where you can share the latest news and information about the extended McDonald family and meet and greet some of your distant cousins.

NOTES

CHAPTER 1

[1] Laurence Overmire, *A Revolutionary American Family: The McDonalds of Somerset County, New Jersey* (Indelible Mark Publishing, 2015).

[2] The 1773 birth date came from *Early New Netherlands Settlers* by Robert Gordon Clarke, ancestry.com, accessed Aug 2013.

[3] Oakwood Cemetery, Troy, NY Interments, US GenWeb Project, accessed Sep 2015. The cemetery record says Richard, son of Richard and Catherine McDonald, died at 50 years of age on Dec 20, 1812, putting his birth date in 1762. Catharine (Rosbrugh McCrea) McDonald was actually Richard's stepmother. His birth mother, Margrietje Schamp McDonald, died in 1773 when Richard was about 11 years old. The cemetery record also confirms that Richard was from New Jersey. A death notice in the *Lansingburgh Gazette* dated Dec 22, 1812, however, says Richard was 51 years of age when he died. That would make his birth year 1761. This date seems less likely, however, because Richard's brother William was born Jan. 18, 1761. If Richard was indeed born in 1761, it probably would have been late in the year in November or December.

[4] Alexander Macrae, *History of the Clan Macrae, with Genealogies* (Dingwall: George Souter, 1910).

[5] Abraham Van Doren Honeyman, ed., *Somerset County Historical Quarterly* (Somerset County Historical Society, Somerville, NJ), Vol 7, 94.

[6] Ibid.

[7] Legend has portrayed Jane "Jennie" McCrea as the "Bride of Fort Edward." She was the daughter of Rev. James McCrea by his first wife, Mary Graham.

[8] Abraham Messler, *Centennial History of Somerset County* (C.M. Jameson, Somerville, NJ, 1878).

[9] L. Overmire, *A Revolutionary American Family,* 18-19. See also *Royal Gazette,* New York, Dec 19, 1778, and *New York Gazette and Weekly Mercury* of the same date.

[10] Ibid, *A Revolutionary American Family,* 20-21.

[11] Ibid, 22-23.

[12] Ibid.

[13] Richard and Catharine's first child, Richard L., was born about 1789. Catharine would have been about 18-20 years old in 1788.

[14] Levinus Lansing is referred to as "Esquire" in the probate records of his son-in-law, Richard McDonald.

[15] Cuyler Reynolds, *Hudson-Mohawk Genealogical and Family Memoirs* (Lewis Historical Publishing Co., 1911), Vol 1, 79.

[16] George Baker Anderson, "History of Lansingburgh, New York," from *Landmarks of Rensselaer County* (D. Mason & Co., Syracuse, NY, 1897), history.rays-place.com, accessed Oct 2015.

[17] Ibid.

[18] Ibid. See also H. J. French, *Historical and Statistical Gazetteer of New York State,* 1860; Town of Lansingburgh, USGenWebProject.

[19] G. B. Anderson, "History of Lansingburgh, New York."

[20] The Lansingburgh Historical Society, lansingburghhistoricalsociety.org, accessed Oct 2015.

[21] Oakwood Cemetery, Troy, NY Interments. See also the death notices for Richard and Catharine McDonald in the *Lansingburgh Gazette,* Dec 22 and 29, 1812, Troy Irish Genealogy Society, rootsweb.ancestry.com, accessed Sept 2015.

[22] *New York, Wills and Probate Records, 1659-1999.*

[23] C. Reynolds, *Hudson-Mohawk Genealogical and Family Memoirs,* 79-80.

[24] *New York, Wills and Probate Records, 1659-1999.*

[25] Ibid. Hester Lansing Allen, the sister of Catharine Lansing McDonald, bequeathed $50 each to Richard, Jacob, Edward, and George McDonald in 1844. Richard, Jacob and George were her nephews, but Edward has not been identified. Since her nephew Lansing McDonald was not bequeathed any money and is presumed to have been alive at the time, it could be that Edward was a first or middle name for him. It does not seem likely that Edward would have been a grandson of Levinus and purposely omitted from his will in 1829.

[26] 1820 federal census, Lansingburgh, Rensselaer, NY.

[27] Rensselaer County Surrogate Court Index, Troy Irish Genealogy Society, rootsweb.ancestry.com, accessed Oct 2015.

[28] *New York, Wills and Probate Records, 1659-1999.*

[29] 1850 federal census, Troy, Rensselaer, NY. Lansing's age on the document is difficult to read. It could be 40 or 60 years old. Either of those would be somewhat off given what we know. However, census records can be notoriously inaccurate when it comes to birth years.

[30] *New York, Wills and Probate Records, 1659-1999.*

[31] Ibid.

[32] Ibid.

[33] Clan Donald USA Genetic Genealogy Project, dna-project.clan-donald-usa.org. We recommend taking a test for at least 67 markers through FamilyTreeDNA.

[34] *New York, Wills and Probate Records, 1659-1999.*

[35] Oakwood Cemetery, Troy, NY Interments.

[36] *New York, Wills and Probate Records, 1659-1999.*

CHAPTER 2

[37] 1850 federal census, Lansingburgh, Rensselaer, NY; *New York, State Census, 1855.*

[38] *New York, Wills and Probate Records, 1659-1999.*

[39] The children are identified in the probate records of their maternal grandfather, Levinus Van Arnum, Mar 11, 1850 (*New York, Wills and Probate Records, 1659-1999*).

[40] 1820 federal census, Lansingburgh, Rensselaer, NY.

[41] Oakwood Cemetery, Troy, NY Interments.

[42] *Lansingburgh Gazette,* Aug 18, 1829, Lansingburgh Marriages, Troy Irish Genealogy Society, rootsweb.ancestry.com, accessed Oct 2015.

[43] *New York, State Census, 1855.*

[44] Frances D. Broderick, *The burial grounds of Lansingburgh, Rensselaer County, New York* (F. D. Broderick, Lansingburgh, N.Y, 1965), 69.

[45] Ibid, 62-63. Text:"In memory of Eldridge, son of Richard and Susan McDonald, died Feb 15 1834, 3 (or 2) yrs, 8 mos." Eldridge was buried in the Lansingburgh Village Cemetery.

[46] 1850 federal census, Lansingburgh, Rensselaer, NY.

[47] G. B. Anderson, "History of Lansingburgh, New York."

[48] 1860 federal census, Lansingburgh, Rensselaer, NY.

[49] *New York, Wills and Probate Records, 1659-1999.*

[50] The birth date comes from the 1870 federal census, Troy Ward 3, Rensselaer, NY.

[51] She is identified as Catherine Ransom in the probate records of her grandfather, Levinus Van Arnum, dated Mar 11, 1850 (*New York, Wills and Probate Records, 1659-1999*).

[52] *Lansingburgh Democrat,* Aug 2, 1855, Lansingburgh Marriages, Troy Irish Genealogy Society.

[53] Lot's will was dated May 21, 1858. He signed a codicil dated Mar 21, 1865. He died before May 19, 1865 when the next probate record was written noting he was deceased (*New York, Wills and Probate Records, 1659-1999*).

[54] Death Records and Obituaries with Troy, NY connections, extracted from a file of Troy, NY newspaper clippings maintained by employees of the Burden Iron Company from Mar 1890 – Apr 1895, Troy Irish Genealogy Society, rootsweb.ancestry.com, accessed Oct 2015.

[55] *New York, State Census, 1855.*

[56] *Lansingburgh Advertiser,* Feb 15, 1840, Lansingburgh Marriages, Troy Irish Genealogy Society.

[57] Troy Burial Records 1842, transcribed by Dottie Kakule, USGenWeb Project, rootsweb.ancestry.com, accessed Oct 5, 2015.

[58] Troy NY *Budget,* Sep 9, 1942, Fulton History, fultonhistory.com, accessed Oct 5, 2015.

[59] *New York, State Census, 1855.*

[60] Death Records and Obituaries with Troy, NY connections, extracted from a file of Troy, NY newspaper clippings maintained by employees of the Burden Iron Company from Mar 1890 – Apr 1895, Troy Irish Genealogy Society.

[61] *Lansingburgh Advertiser,* Jan 11, 1840, Lansingburgh Marriages, Troy Irish Genealogy Society.

[62] 1850 federal census, Lansingburgh, Rensselaer, NY.

[63] *New York, State Census, 1855.*

[64] Leonard Ransom mentioned his friend James B. Smith in his will (*New York, Wills and Probate Records, 1659-1999*). Sidney's middle name was probably bestowed in honor of this Smith family.

[65] 1860 federal census, Schaghticoke, Rensselaer, NY.

[66] *New York, State Census, 1865.*

[67] 1870 federal census, Monroe, Colusa, CA.

[68] 1880 federal census, Oakland, Alameda, CA.

[69] *California, Voter Registers, 1866-1898.* This record shows his middle name as "Smith."

[70] 1900 federal census, San Francisco, San Francisco, CA.

[71] 1910 federal census, Oakland, Alameda, CA.

[72] *U.S. City Directories, 1822-1989.*

[73] Her name is also spelled Calouise in some records. The 1900 federal census for San Francisco says she was born Sept 1872. Census records are often inaccurate when it comes to birth dates, however.

[74] *California, Death Index, 1940-1997. California, Voter Registers, 1866-1898* shows Guy's middle name, profession and physical description.

[75] Guy's grandfather William Calden (b. abt 1818, NH) may have been the brother of Caloise's grandfather, Alburn Calden (b. abt 1823, NH).

[76] 1870 federal census, Monroe, Colusa, CA.

[77] *California, Military Registers, 1858-1923.*

[78] Guy passed his legal examinations in 1899 ("Twenty Six New Attorneys," *San Francisco Call,* Vol 85, No 151, Apr 30, 1999).

[79] 1900 federal census, San Francisco, San Francisco, CA.

[80] 1910 federal census, Oakland, Alameda, CA.

[81] Death notice of Mrs. C. R. Calden, *Oakland Tribune,* Oakland, CA, Aug 17, 1910.

[82] *California, Death Index, 1940-1997.*

[83] Ibid.

[84] *U.S., School Yearbooks, 1880-2012.*

[85] *California, Marriage Records from Select Counties, 1850-1941.*

[86] The 1930 federal census for San Francisco shows Reed was a World War I veteran.

[87] *U.S., World War I Draft Registration Cards, 1917-1918.*

[88] *California, Death Index, 1940-1997.* Reed's WWI draft registration shows he was born in Clinton. His WWII registration shows he was born in Croley.

[89] *San Francisco City-County Record*, Jan-Feb, 1955, 6.

[90] *California Birth Index, 1905-1995.*

[91] *California, Death Index, 1940-1997.*

[92] *U.S., Social Security Applications and Claims Index, 1936-2007.*

[93] *U.S., School Yearbooks, 1880-2012.*

[94] *U.S., Social Security Applications and Claims Index, 1936-2007.*

[95] Sgt. Bill Conroy, Biography of Jack Tucker, marinechat.com, accessed Oct 6, 2015.

[96] Ibid.

[97] Ibid.

[98] Ibid.

[99] *U.S., Social Security Death Index, 1935-2014.*

[100] B. Conroy, Biography of Jack Tucker.

[101] Ibid.

[102] *U.S., Social Security Applications and Claims Index, 1936-2007.*

[103] B. Conroy, Biography of Jack Tucker.

[104] Ibid.

[105] He is referred to as Guy C. Calden Jr. in some records.

[106] *U.S. Passport Applications, 1795-1925.*

[107] *California, Marriage Records from Select Counties, 1850-1941; California, Death Index, 1940-1997;* 1940 federal census, Fresno, Fresno, CA.

[108] 1930 federal census, South Pasadena, Los Angeles, CA; 1940 federal census, Fresno, Fresno, CA. The 1930 census shows Guy was a World War I veteran.

[109] *California, Marriage Index, 1960-1985; California Birth Index, 1905-1995.* Gertrude's maiden name was Beckwith.

[110] *California, Death Index, 1940-1997.*

[111] *U.S., Social Security Death Index, 1935-2014;* Find A Grave Memorial #86793961.

[112] The 1900 federal census for San Francisco, San Francisco, CA, show her birth date as Aug. 1882.

[113] Ladewig Family Tree, Owner: BrianLadewig, ancestry.com, accessed Oct 2015.

[114] *U.S., World War I Draft Registration Cards, 1917-1918; California, Death Index, 1940-1997.*

[115] *California, Death Index, 1940-1997.*

[116] Ibid.

[117] *California, Marriage Records from Select Counties, 1850-1941.*

[118] *California, Death Index, 1940-1997; U.S., World War II Draft Registration Cards, 1942.*

[119] *U.S., World War II Draft Registration Cards, 1942.*

[120] *California, Death Index, 1940-1997.*

[121] Ibid.

[122] 1940 federal census, Oakland, Alameda, CA.

[123] GoodmanNormand Family Tree, Owner: JamesGoodman1957, ancestry.com, accessed Oct 2015.

[124] *California, Death Index, 1940-1997.*

[125] Ibid.

[126] *California Birth Index, 1905-1995.*

[127] Kenneth Flory, Flory Family Tree, floryfamilytree.com, accessed Oct 2015; *California, Marriage Index, 1949-1959.*

[128] Ibid.

[129] Obituary of Edward G. Ladewig, *The Bridgeport Post*, Bridgeport, CT, Mar 2, 1974, 22; *U.S., Social Security Death Index, 1935-2014.*

[130] Ibid.

[131] Ladewig Family Tree.

[132] *Connecticut Death Index, 1949-2012.*

[133] Obituary of Edward G. Ladewig.

[134] *Connecticut Death Index, 1949-2012.*

[135] Obituary of Edward G. Ladewig.

[136] *California, Death Index, 1940-1997.*

[137] Ibid.

[138] Ibid.

[139] Find a Grave Memorial #148837228.

[140] *California, Death Index, 1940-1997; California Birth Index, 1905-1995.*

[141] Death notice of Cornelius McDonald, *Lansingburgh Gazette*, Jun 22, 1849, Troy Irish Genealogy Society.

[142] *New York, Wills and Probate Records, 1659-1999.*

[143] 1900 federal census, Lansingburgh, Rensselaer, NY; New York, State Census, 1855.

[144] *Lansingburgh Gazette,* Jan 3, 1860, Lansingburgh Marriages, Troy Irish Genealogy Society.

[145] The middle initial "D" may have stood for Drummer. George died on July 24, 1872, in Lansingburgh, at the age of 4y 7m, and was buried in Oakwood Cemetery (Oakwood Cemetery, Troy, NY Interments). Calculating accordingly, George's birth date would have been Dec. 22, 1867, if the record is accurate.

[146] Angie B. McDonald died on Apr 13, 1873, in Lansingburgh at 8m of age (Oakwood Cemetery, Troy, NY Interments).

[147] Burden Iron Works Marriage Records, Marriage Records with Troy, NY area connections, Troy Irish Genealogy Society.

[148] *U.S., World War I Draft Registration Cards, 1917-1918.*

[149] Stapf Family Tree, Owner: AmandaArze, ancestry.com, accessed Oct 2015.

[150] Ibid.

[151] *U.S., World War I Draft Registration Cards, 1917-1918.*

[152] Ibid.

[153] Harry Cohen, *Albany's Part in the World War* (Forgotten Books, London, 2013, originally published 1919), 124. Text: "MacDonald, R. E., 429 Third street, 248th Aero Squadron, A. E. F., Sergeant." See also Stapf Family Tree.

[154] Col. Edgar S. Gorrell, *History of the American Expeditionary Forces Air Service, 1917-1919*, Vol 22.

[155] Stapf Family Tree.

[156] 1900 federal census, Albany Ward 3, Albany, NY; Stapf Family Tree.

[157] 1930 federal census, Bethlehem, Albany, NY.

[158] *U.S., Social Security Death Index, 1935-2014.*

[159] Obituary of Margaret Schafer MacDonald from an unknown newspaper, courtesy of Stapf Family Tree.

[160] *U.S., Social Security Applications and Claims Index, 1936-2007.*

[161] *U.S. Veterans Gravesites, ca.1775-2006.*

[162] *Florida Death Index, 1877-1998.*

[163] Ibid.

[164] Ibid.

[165] Find A Grave Memorial #76542818.

[166] *U.S., Find A Grave Index, 1600s-Current.*

[167] Find A Grave Memorial #76542879.

[168] *U.S., Social Security Applications and Claims Index, 1936-2007.*

[169] Stapf Family Tree.

[170] Ibid.

[171] *U.S. World War II Navy Muster Rolls, 1938-1949.*

[172] *U.S., Department of Veterans Affairs BIRLS Death File, 1850-2010.*

[173] Andrew Toppan, Haze Gray & Underway, Naval History and Photography, hazegray.org, accessed Nov 2015; "Wilson (DD 408)," Destroyer History Foundation, destroyerhistory.org, accessed Nov 2015.

[174] Coincidentally, Raymond E. Overmire Jr., the father of the author of this book, was an ensign aboard the aircraft carrier USS *Bunker Hill* during the Okinawa campaign. His ship was struck by two kamikazes on May 11, 1945, killing 346 sailors and airmen, with 43 missing and 246 wounded. Ensign Overmire was off-duty, below deck when the attack happened and barely escaped with his life.

[175] Ibid.

[176] *U.S. City Directories, 1822-1989.*

[177] Obituary of Frank J. Stapf, *Albany Times Union*, Albany, NY, Apr 6, 2009.

[178] *Florida Death Index, 1877-1998.*

[179] Obituary of Frank J. Stapf.

[180] Ibid.

[181] Obituary of Raymond C. MacDonald, *The Republican*, Springfield, MA, Oct 20, 2011.

[182] Ibid.

---

[183] USS *LSM-216*, *Wikipedia*, accessed Oct 2015.

[184] Wedding announcement of Raymond MacDonald and Ann Burry, *The Knickerbocker News*, Albany, NY, Aug 2, 1947. Some show the surname as "Barry," but most records spell it "Burry" including her father's WWI draft record, which shows he clearly signed his name, "Burry."

[185] Ibid.

[186] *U.S., Social Security Applications and Claims Index, 1936-2007.*

[187] Obituary of Raymond C. MacDonald, *The Republican*, Springfield, MA, Oct 20, 2011.

[188] Ibid.

[189] Find A Grave Memorial #133553736.

[190] Ibid.

[191] If Raymond or his sons match the Y-DNA of other McDonald descendants of Maj. Richard McDonald of Somerset County from other branches of the tree, then all descendants of Richard and Catharine (Lansing) McDonald can be assured that they are, in fact, descended from Maj. Richard. See *A Revolutionary American Family: The McDonalds of Somerset County, New Jersey* for more information on DNA testing as it relates to the Somerset County McDonalds.

[192] *U.S. Public Records Index, 1950-1993, Volume 1.*

[193] *U.S., Social Security Applications and Claims Index, 1936-2007.*

[194] 1940 federal census, Bethleham, Albany, NY.

[195] *U.S. Veterans Gravesites, ca.1775-2006;* Find A Grave Memorial #79496249.

[196] 28th Infantry Regiment, *Wikipedia*, accessed Oct 2015.

[197] Find A Grave Memorial #79496249.

[198] Obituary of Jeanne Frances MacDonald Augustine, Seawright Funeral Home, 2016.

CHAPTER 3

[199] Catharine was at least 21 years of age when her parents died in 1812, as noted in the probate records of her father, Richard (*New York, Wills and Probate Records, 1659-1999*). Text: "The said Levinus Lansing personally appeared & presented his petition setting forth that the said Rich. McDonald died intestate, that his Widow is dead and that all his children & heirs at law are under the age of 21 years except his son Richd L. McDonald & his daughter Catharine the wife of James Adams Esq, and that the Infant heirs of the dec'd have no Guardian."

[200] James Adams is denoted as Esq. in his father-in-law Richard McDonald's probate records (*New York, Wills and Probate Records, 1659-1999*).

[201] 1808 Marriages from the Reformed Dutch Church of the Boght. Text: "24 Jun-James ADAMS and Catharine Mc DONALD." See also Bunline-Boutell Family Tree, Owner: gjsalyer, ancestry.com.

[202] Baptisms at the Schaghticoke Dutch Reformed Church 1752-1866, USGenWeb Project, rootsweb.ancestry.com, accessed Oct 2015; Bunline-Boutell Family Tree.

[203] *New York, Wills and Probate Records, 1659-1999.*

[204] Ibid.

[205] Find A Grave Memorial #16886472. The stone says she died Oct 14, 1840, aged 33 yrs.

[206] Charles V. DeLand, "The De Lamater Family," *DeLand's History of Jackson County, Michigan* (B.F. Bowen, 1903), 358-359; Deb Hayes-Wolfe, Find A Grave Memorial #16886453.

[207] Ibid, 358-359.

[208] Ibid, 358. Anson's brothers were Edward, Abraham and Isaac.

[209] Find A Grave Memorial #16886472.

[210] *Michigan Marriages 1868-1925.*

[211] C. V. DeLand, *DeLand's History of Jackson County, Michigan*, 359.

[212] Find A Grave Memorial #16886472

[213] Oakwood Cemetery Burial Records, microfilm at NYS Library, Albany, NY. Text: " George W Adams died June 22, 1884 at age 77y 5m 10d, born in Lansingburgh to James Adams – record 9523 lot S24."

[214] Barbara Jeffries web page, "Marriages 1st Presbyterian Church of Troy, NY," members.tripod.com. Text: "1836 Jan 21 George W Adams – Lydia H Fowler."

[215] Oakwood Cemetery Burial Records. Text: "Lydia F Adams died March 21, 1889 at age 71y 8m, born in Brunswick to James and Jane Fowler – record 11841 lot S24."

[216] *New York, State Census, 1855.*

[217] Lansingburgh Newspapers 1787-1895, compiled by Troy Public Library, 1939. Text: "Adams, George, W. 73, d. June 22, 1884 L. Cour. June 28, 1884, 3:3."

[218] Oakwood Cemetery Burial Records.

[219] Oakwood Cemetery, Troy, NY Interments.

[220] *New York, State Census, 1855.*

[221] Oakwood Cemetery Burial Records. Text: "Emma Geer died February 5, 1870 at age 23, she was born in Brunswick to George W and Lydia Adams – record 3382 lot S24."

[222] Ellen appears as "Addie" in *New York, State Census, 1855.*

[223] *New York, State Census, 1855.* The 1900 federal census, Buffalo, Erie, NY, shows Ellen born Apr 1854.

[224] 1880 federal census, Troy, Rensselaer, NY.

[225] 1900 federal census, Buffalo, Erie, NY.

[226] *U.S., Social Security Death Index, 1935-2014.*

CHAPTER 4

[227] The Genealogy Wheel of Katherine Hun Peltz (1880-1978) showing the ancestry of John Benjamin Gale and Elizabeth Van Schoonhovan Wells, a family heirloom provided courtesy of Peter Peltz. This document shows Elizabeth McDonald's birth date. It identifies Elizabeth's mother as Catharine Lansing, but it did not identify her father. See also *New York, State Census, 1855.*

[228] L. Overmire, *A Revolutionary American Family: The McDonalds of Somerset County, New Jersey*, 26.

[229] *Lansingburgh Gazette*, Nov 11, 1823, Lansingburgh Marriages, Troy Irish Genealogy Society. The parents of Philander Wells are identified in The Genealogy Wheel of Katherine Hun Peltz.

[230] Oakwood Cemetery, Troy, New York, 1851-1872 Interments, USGenWeb Project, rootsweb.ancestry.com, accessed Oct 2015.

[231] Henry Varnum Poor, *History of the Railroads and Canals of the United States* (John H. Schultz & Co., NY, 1860), 319.

[232] 1870 federal census, Troy, Rensselaer, NY.

[233] *New York, Wills and Probate Records, 1659-1999.* The will was probated Oct 18, 1870.

[234] Oakwood Cemetery Troy, New York 1851-1872 Interments.

[235] Ibid.

[236] *New York, State Census, 1865.*

[237] The middle name "Van Schoonhovan" was identified by The Genealogy Wheel of Katherine Hun Peltz (1880-1978) showing the ancestry of John Benjamin Gale and Elizabeth Van Schoonhovan Wells, a family heirloom provided courtesy of Peter Peltz. The name is alternately spelled "Van Schoonhoven." See also Ulyang Family Tree, Owner: vickieldc, ancestry.com, accessed Oct 2015.

[238] Her birth date is noted on The Genealogy Wheel of Katherine Hun Peltz; *New York, State Census, 1865.*

[239] C. Reynolds, *Hudson-Mohawk Genealogical and Family Memoirs*, Vol 1, 199.

[240] *U.S. Passport Applications, 1795-1925.*

[241] 1850 federal census, Troy, Rensselaer, NY.

[242] *U.S. Passport Applications, 1795-1925.*

[243] The Genealogy Wheel of Katherine Hun Peltz; Oakwood Cemetery, Troy, NY Interments.

[244] Elizabeth's husband, John B. Gale was issued a passport on Sept. 9, 1871. He intended to go abroad with his daughter and his niece. Elizabeth, sadly, was deceased by then or she might have gone on the trip. John married his second wife, Catherine J. Wells, in 1872.

[245] *U.S. Passport Applications, 1795-1925.*

[246] *Massachusetts, Death Records, 1841-1915.*

[247] Find A Grave Memorial #108199249.

[248] *U.S., Find A Grave Index, 1600s-Current; New York, Passenger Lists, 1820-1957.*

[249] William Horace Eliot Jr., *Genealogy of the Descendants of John Eliot, "Apostle to the Indians," 1598-1905* (Tuttle, Morehouse & Taylor Press, New Haven, CT, 1905), 45.

[250] Ibid.

[251] Henry Mills Hurd, Biography of Dr. Edward Reynolds Hun, *The Institutional Care of the Insane in the United States and Canada* (The John Hopkins Press, Baltimore, MD, 1917), Vol 4, 428-429.

[252] H. M. Hurd, *The Institutional Care of the Insane*, 428.

[253] C. Reynolds, *Hudson-Mohawk Genealogical and Family Memoirs*, Vol 1, 198-199.

[254] Obituary of Edward Reynolds Hun, *Catalogue of the Alumni, Officers and Fellows, 1807-1891*, 92, Columbia University Medical Center, Archives and Special Collections, library-archives.cumc.columbia.edu, accessed Oct 2015.

[255] H. M. Hurd, *The Institutional Care of the Insane*, 428.

[256] C. Reynolds, *Hudson-Mohawk Genealogical and Family Memoirs*, Vol 1, 199.

[257] Ibid.

[258] H. M. Hurd, *The Institutional Care of the Insane*, 429; *U.S. Federal Census Mortality Schedules, 1850-1885.*

[259] Find A Grave Memorial #102397619.

[260] C. Reynolds, *Hudson-Mohawk Genealogical and Family Memoirs*, Vol 1, 199.

[261] Ibid.

[262] Ibid. See also 1880 federal census, Toledo, Lucas, OH.

[263] *U.S. Passport Applications, 1795-1925.*

[264] *The Ten-Year Book of the Cornell University, 1868-1898*, Vol 3, 81.

[265] Obituary of Frederick Williams Kelley, "The Cornell Alumni News," Oct 1932, Vol xxxv, No. 2, 19.

[266] Ibid.

[267] Ibid.

[268] *U.S. Passport Applications, 1795-1925.*

[269] Obituary of Frederick Williams Kelley.

[270] *Menands, New York, Albany Rural Cemetery Burial Cards, 1791-2011.*

[271] Find A Grave Memorial #125903927.

[272] *Menands, New York, Albany Rural Cemetery Burial Cards, 1791-2011.*

[273] *Wisconsin, Births and Christenings Index, 1826-1908;* Lance Family Tree, Owner: 1_kromine, ancestry.com, accessed Oct 2015.

[274] *Wisconsin, Births and Christenings Index, 1826-1908.*

[275] *New York, Military Service Cards, 1816-1979.*

[276] Ibid. See also *U.S., Select Military Registers, 1862-1985.*

[277] *Menands, New York, Albany Rural Cemetery Burial Cards, 1791-2011.*

[278] Find A Grave Memorial #142612215.

[279] Obituary of A. Brooks Harlow Jr., Craig Funeral Home, St. Augustine, FL, 2014.

[280] Obituary of Miriam (Mimi) Baxter Harlow, *Darien News*, Darien, CT, Oct 8, 2015.

[281] *The Michigan Alumnus* (The Alumni Association of the University of Michigan, Ann Arbor, MI), Vol LXVI, 92.

[282] Obituary of A. Brooks Harlow Jr.

[283] Obituary of Miriam (Mimi) Baxter Harlow.

[284] Obituary of A. Brooks Harlow Jr.

[285] C. Reynolds, *Hudson-Mohawk Genealogical and Family Memoirs*, Vol 1, 199.

[286] *Menands, New York, Albany Rural Cemetery Burial Cards, 1791-2011.*

[287] *Cornellian Yearbook*, Cornell University, Class of 1929, e-yearbook.com.

[288] Ibid.

[289] Find A Grave Memorial #125903733.

[290] *U.S. Passport Applications, 1795-1925.*

[291] *Encyclopedia of American Biography* (The American Historical Society, 1928), Vol XXXV.

[292] For the complete history of the McDonald ancestors, see L. Overmire's *A Revolutionary American Family: The McDonalds of Somerset County, New Jersey.*

[293] *Massachusetts, Marriage Records, 1840-1915.*

[294] C. Reynolds, *Hudson-Mohawk Genealogical and Family Memoirs*, Vol 1, 199.

[295] *Encyclopedia of American Biography.*

[296] The Hun School of Princeton, hunschool.org, accessed Oct 2015.

[297] *Menands, New York, Albany Rural Cemetery Burial Cards, 1791-2011.*

[298] Find A Grave Memorial #102260584.

[299] *Pennsylvania, Death Certificates, 1906-1963.*

[300] John Stover Arndt, *The Story of the Arndts: The Life, Antecedents and Descendants of Bernhard Arndt Who Emigrated to Pennsylvania in the Year 1731* (Christopher Sower Co., Philadelphia, 1922), 398.

[301] *Pennsylvania, Death Certificates, 1906-1963.*

[302] Obituary of Edward Shippen Morris, *Princeton Alumni Weekly*, Sept 18, 1959, Vol 60, 35.

[303] John Stover Arndt, *The Story of the Arndts*, 398.

[304] *Princeton Alumni Weekly*, Sept 26, 1930, Vol 31, 806.

[305] Obituary of Edward Shippen Morris, *Princeton Alumni Weekly*, Sept 18, 1959, Vol 60, 35.

[306] Ibid.

[307] *Pennsylvania, Death Certificates, 1906-1963.*

[308] Find A Grave Memorial #103823315.

[309] *Princeton Alumni Weekly*, Feb 25, 1955, Vol 55, 15.

[310] Ibid. See also *California, Marriage Records from Select Counties, 1850-1941.*

[311] Biography and resume of Roland Morris, Duane Morris LLP, duanemorris.com, accessed Oct 2015.

[312] C. Reynolds, *Hudson-Mohawk Genealogical and Family Memoirs*, Vol 1, 199.

[313] *Sweet Briar College, Alumnae Magazine 1936-40*, 15.

[314] *Cook County, Illinois, Birth Certificates Index, 1871-1922.*

[315] History of The Hun School of Princeton, hunschool.org, accessed Oct 2015.

[316] *U.S., Social Security Death Index, 1935-2014* and Find A Grave Memorial #171382704

[317] Find A Grave Memorial #171380751

[318] Mrs. Gordon M. Baker, Virginia Profiles, virginiaprofiles.com, accessed Oct 2015.

[319] Gordon McAllen Baker, Facebook page, facebook.com, accessed Oct 2015.

[320] Obituary of Susan Hun McAllen Turner, *Lake Placid News*, NY, July 22, 2005, 7.

[321] Ibid.

[322] 1940 federal census, Anniston, Calhoun, AL.

[323] *U.S., School Yearbooks, 1880-2012.*

[324] *U.S., Social Security Death Index, 1935-2014*; OHernMorrisWardlaw Genealogy, ohernmorris.com, accessed Oct 2015.

[325] Hugh T. Patrick, *Archives of Neurology and Psychiatry* (American Medical Association, Chicago, IL, 1919) Vol 1, 10; *U.S., Civil War Soldier Records and Profiles, 1861-1865.*

[326] 1940 federal census, Anniston, Calhoun, AL.

[327] *Massachusetts Death Index, 1970-2003.*

[328] Death notice of Leslie Stafford Crawford Hun, *The New York Times*, July 23, 1964.

[329] *U.S., Social Security Applications and Claims Index, 1936-2007.*

[330] C. Reynolds, *Hudson-Mohawk Genealogical and Family Memoirs*, Vol 1, 199.

[331] William Buell Sprague, *Annals of the American Pulpit:; or Commemorative Notices of Distinguished American Clergymen of Various Denominations* (Robert Carter and Brothers, New York, 1869), Vol 9, 177.

[332] L. Overmire, *A Revolutionary American Family: The McDonalds of Somerset County, New Jersey.*

[333] G. Elton Parks, *Sexennial Record of the Class of 1904 Yale College* (Yale University Press, 1911), 901.

[334] Find A Grave Memorial #142606990.

[335] *U.S., Social Security Applications and Claims Index, 1936-2007.*

[336] Ibid.

[337] "Chester Kerr, editor emeritus of the Yale University Press, dies," Yale Bulletin & Calendar, Sept 6-13, 1999, Vol 28, No. 3. Chester died on Oct 22, 1999, at the age of 86.

[338] Chester Brooks Kerr died on Aug. 22, 1999, aged 86. He was buried in Riverside Cemetery, Norwalk, Fairfield, CT (Find A Grave Memorial #139713314).

[339] The quote is an inscription on his tombstone (Find A Grave Memorial #99335544).

[340] Find A Grave Memorial #99335544.

[341] Obituary of Caroline Peltz Schultze, PostStar.com, June 5, 2007.

[342] Find A Grave Memorial #71265982.

[343] Philip Kerr papers 1984-2012, Michigan Historical Collections, Bentley Historical Library, University of Michigan, quod.lib.umich.edu, accessed Oct 2015.

[344] Fiona Gregory, "Crossing Genre, Age and Gender: Judith Anderson as Hamlet," *The Journal of American Drama and Theatre* (Spring 2014), Vol 26, No. 2, CUNY Academic Commons.

[345] Philip Kerr biography, *Michigan Muse*, University of Michigan, Fall 2012, Vol 7, No. 1.

[346] Philip Kerr papers 1984-2012.

[347] Sarah-Jane Gwillim, University of Michigan, School of Musit, Theatre and Danece, music.umich.edu, accessed Oct 2015; Sarah-Jane Gwillim, *Wikipedia*, accessed Oct 2015.

[348] Philip Kerr biography, *Michigan Muse*.

[349] William H. Peltz, correspondence with Laurence Overmire, Nov 2015.

[350] Obituary of William L. Peltz, M.D., *Vineyard Gazette*, Martha's Vineyard, MA, Sept 28, 2003, vineyardgazette.com; *U.S., School Yearbooks, 1880-2012.*

[351] *New Hampshire, Marriage and Divorce Records, 1659-1947.*

[352] *U.S., Social Security Applications and Claims Index, 1936-2007.*

[353] Lewis Perry (1877-1970) biography, Archives & Special Collections, Williams College, archives.williams.edu, accessed Oct 2015.

[354] Obituary of William L. Peltz, M.D.

[355] *Massachusetts Death Index, 1970-2003.*

[356] Ibid.

[357] Find A Grave Memorial #93463259.

[358] Obituary of William L. Peltz, M.D.

[359] W. H. Peltz, correspondence with L. Overmire.

[360] Ibid.

[361] Ibid.

[362] Ibid.

[363] Missy Peltz, LinkedIn, linkedin.com, accessed Nov 2015.

[364] Jennifer Peltz McCurley, Facebook, facebook.com; W. H. Peltz, correspondence with L. Overmire.

[365] *U.S., Social Security Applications and Claims Index, 1936-2007.*

[366] Obituary of Dr. Theodore Burg Russell, *Princeton Alumni Weekly*, Feb 9, 1971, Vol 71, 16.

[367] Ibid.

[368] Obituary of Lewis Perry Jr., *Vineyard Gazette*, Martha's Vineyard, MA, Aug 12, 2010; Phoebe MacAdams Ozuna, correspondence with Laurence Overmire, Nov 17, 2015.

[369] Lewis Perry Sr.'s stepdaughter, Margaret Ruth Adams, married Dr. William Learned Peltz, the elder brother of Mary Learned Peltz.

[370] Obituary of Lewis Perry Jr.

[371] Ibid.

[372] *U.S., Social Security Death Index, 1935-2014.*

[373] Obituary of Dr. Theodore Burg Russell, *Princeton Alumni Weekly*, Feb 9, 1971, Vol 71, 16.

[374] Find A Grave Memorial #82955646.

[375] Obituary of Lewis Perry Jr., *Vineyard Gazette*, Martha's Vineyard, MA, Aug 12, 2010.

[376] Katherine Learned White Marsland, correspondence with Laurence Overmire, Nov 2015.

[377] Richard Booth White, Prabook, prabook.org, accessed Oct 2015.

[378] Obituary of Richard Booth White, *New Canaan Advertiser*, New Canaan, CT, Apr. 30, 2014.

[379] Richard Booth White, Prabook.

[380] K. L. W. Marsland, correspondence with L. Overmire.

[381] Obituary of Richard Booth White.

[382] K. L. W. Marsland, correspondence with L. Overmire.

[383] Ibid; Richard Booth White, Prabook.

384 K. L. W. Marsland, correspondence with L. Overmire.

385 Southern Connecticut University, southernct.edu, accessed Oct 2015.

[386] K. L. W. Marsland, correspondence with L. Overmire.

[387] Bill O'Brien, "The World, Through Michael Marsland's Lens," *Branford Eagle*, Branford, CT, Aug 6, 2015.

[388] Ibid.

[389] Ibid.

[390] Leslie White-Siek, Linked In, linkedin.com, accessed Oct 2015.

[391] Leslie White-Siek, correspondence with Laurence Overmire, Nov 29, 2015.

[392] L. White-Siek, LinkedIn.

[393] L. White-Siek, correspondence with L. Overmire.

[394] Phoebe MacAdams Ozuna, correspondence with Laurence Overmire, Nov 17, 2015.

[395] Benno C. Schmidt Jr., *Wikipedia*, accessed Oct 2015.

[396] Ibid.

[397] Weddings, Elizabeth Schmidt and Eric Liftin, *The New York Times*, Oct 6, 1996.

[398] Phoebe MacAdams Ozuna, correspondence with Laurence Overmire, Nov 2015.

[399] Ibid.

[400] Weddings, Elizabeth Schmidt and Eric Liftin, *The New York Times*; Elizabeth Schmidt, LinkedIn, linkedin.com, accessed Oct 2015.

[401] Eric Liftin, LinkedIn, linkedin.com, accessed Oct 2015.

[402] E. Schmidt, LinkedIn.

[403] Goodreads, goodreads.com, accessed Oct 2015.

[404] The Poets Laureate Anthology, amazon.com, accessed Oct 2015.

[405] E. Schmidt, LinkedIn.

[406] Betsey Schmidt bio, Mesh Ed, meshed.org, accessed Feb 2021.

[407] Ms. Phoebe Ozuna – Pasadena, California, California Public Profiles, californiaprofiles.com, accessed Oct 2015.

[408] Lewis MacAdams papers, SMU, Texas Archival Resources Online, lib.utexas.edu, accessed Oct 2015.

[409] Dale Smith, "Dale Smith reviews Lewis MacAdams," Jacket Magazine, jacketmagazine.com, accessed Oct 2015.

[410] Lewis MacAdams papers, SMU.

[411] P. M. Ozuna, correspondence with L. Overmire.

[412] Bill Mohr, "Phoebe MacAdams on Teaching," Bill Mohr's website, billmohrpoet.com, accessed Oct 2015.

[413] P. M. Ozuna, correspondence with L. Overmire.

[414] "Phoebe MacAdams: Four Poems," *Cultural Weekly*, culturalweekly.com, accessed Oct 2015.

[415] Phoebe MacAdams bio, Cahuenga Press, cahuengapress.com, accessed Oct 2015.

416 B. Mohr, "Phoebe MacAdams on Teaching."

417 "Phoebe MacAdams: Four Poems," *Cultural Weekly*.

418 P. M. Ozuna, correspondence with L. Overmire.

419 *California Birth Index, 1905-1995*.

420 Ocean MacAdams, Linked In, linkedin.com, accessed Oct 2015.

421 Ibid; Ocean MacAdams, facebook.com, accessed Oct 2015.

422 Susanne Petren-Moritz, linkedin.com, accessed Oct 2015.

423 P. M. Ozuna, correspondence with L. Overmire, Nov 11, 2015.

424 *California Birth Index, 1905-1995*.

425 *U.S., School Yearbooks, 1880-2012*.

426 Resumé of Will MacAdams, willmacadams.com, accessed Oct 2015.

427 Ibid.

428 Resumé of Mikiko Suzuki MacAdams, Set Design, mikikosuzukimacadams.com, accessed Oct 2015.

429 *Vermont, Death Records, 1909-2008*.

430 Whiffs of 1938, Yale Whiffenpoof Alumni, Inc., Media Library, whiffalumni.com, accessed Oct 2015.

431 Obituary of Philip Peltz, *Cape Cod Times*, Hyannis, MA, Apr 2, 2001.

432 Ibid. See also *U.S. World War II Navy Muster Rolls, 1938-1949*.

433 *Vermont, Death Records, 1909-2008*.

434 Obituary of Philip Peltz.

435 Joseph H. Ellis, *Birds in Wood and Paint: American Miniature Bird Carvings and Their Carvers, 1900-1970* (University Press of New England, 2009), 165.

436 Shawnee Peltz Unger, correspondence with Laurence Overmire, Nov 23, 2015.

437 Ibid.

438 Obituary of Philip Peltz.

439 S. P. Unger, correspondence with L. Overmire.

440 *Vermont, Death Records, 1909-2008*.

441 Peter Peltz's Biography, Vote Smart, votesmart.org, accessed Oct 2015.

442 Obituary of Doris Gantt, *The Seattle Times*, Seattle, WA, May 13, 2012.

443 Obituary of Benjamin J. Gantt Jr. (1922-2009), *The Seattle Times*, Seattle, WA, Jun 28, 2009.

444 Cacky Gantt Peltz, Art Teacher, Stowe Elementary School, zoominfo.com, accessed Oct 2015.

445 Vermont Agency of Education, Committee of Practitioners, Minutes of Meeting, May 8, 2015, education.vermont.gov, accessed Oct 2015.

446 OSSU School Boards, Woodbury School Board Members, sites.google.com, accessed Oct 2015.

447 Peter Peltz's Biography, Vote Smart.

448 Representative Peter Peltz, legislature.vermont.gov, accessed Oct 2015.

449 Town Hill Pottery, The Studios of Aysha Peltz & Todd Wahlstrom, townhillpottery.com, accessed Oct 2015.

450 Bennington Faculty, bennington.edu, accessed Oct 2015.

451 Aysha Peltz Ceramics, facebook.com, accessed Oct 2015.

452 Obituary of Doris Gantt, *The Seattle Times*, Seattle, WA, May 13, 2012.

453 About Peltz Creative, peltzcreative.com, accessed Oct 2015.

454 Ann Peltz biography, Peltz Creative, peltzcreative.com, accessed Oct 2015.

455 Alex Peltz biography, Peltz Creative, peltzcreative.com, accessed Oct 2015.

456 S. P. Unger, correspondence with L. Overmire.

457 Ibid.

458 Ibid.

459 Ibid.

[460] Ibid.

[461] Ibid.

[462] The middle name "Van Schoonhovan" was identified by Ulvang Family Tree, ancestry.com, accessed Oct 2015.

[463] *U.S., Find A Grave Index, 1600s-Current.*

[464] Find A Grave Memorial #108199249.

CHAPTER 5

[465] William's story is told in another e-book by this author, *William R. McDonald and Abigail Fowler of Herkimer County, New York & Their Descendants* (Indelible Mark Publishing, 2015).

[466] Michael John and Thomas Corey each tested for 67 markers. They matched with a genetic distance of 2. FamilyTreeDNA shows that the results for 67 markers with a genetic distance of 2 has an 85.25% probability that Michael John McDonald and Thomas Corey McDonald share a common ancestor within 8 generations. The paper trails for these two men, however, tell us exactly who that common ancestor is – Maj. Richard McDonald of Somerset County, NJ.

CHAPTER 6

[467] Peter Macdonald Blachly (aka Peter Alexander), correspondence with Laurence Overmire, Nov 17, 2016.

[468] Death notice and tribute to Mary Antoinette deWitt, by J.H.B. from a newspaper clipping (source unknown) included in an envelope dated July 13, 1945, in the files of Peter Macdonald Blachly and transcribed by Laurence Overmire, Nov. 2016. The envelope was addressed to Mrs. William A. Howell (Katharine Macdonald Howell). A notation in pencil noted "This Tribute written by cousin Jaelin or Julia? Hastronato? Bruin?, Kingston, NY."

[469] Correspondence with Shawn Marchinek, Apr. 25, 2019.

[470] Find A Grave Memorial #61515756.

INDEX

O

About the Author

Laurence Overmire has had a multi-faceted career as an actor, director, poet, author, educator, genealogist and lecturer. He received a B.A. and B.S. from Muskingum University and an M.F.A. from the University of Minnesota. As an actor, he has performed on stage and screen in New York, Hollywood and points in between, most notably in *Amadeus* on Broadway and in the television soaps *All My Children* and *Loving*. He was also executive producer for The Writer's Lab, a non-profit organization in Hollywood to promote quality script writing for the entertainment industry.

Overmire is the author of five books of poetry as well as an inspirational work recently published in a second edition titled, *The One Idea That Saves The World: A Message of Hope in a Time of Crisis*. It has been widely acclaimed for its compassionate, common sense approach to many of the world's most pressing issues.

Overmire has spent much of the last three decades immersed in genealogical and historical research, creating several genealogical reference databases on Rootsweb.com including *The Ancestry of Overmire, Tifft, Richardson, Bradford, Reed*, which has helped hundreds of thousands of people trace their family trees and find their connections to famous historical figures. He also maintains over 2,600 memorials on Find A Grave.

Overmire's thorough investigation of his paternal ancestry culminated in the publication of *One Immigrant's Legacy: The Overmyer Family in America, 1751-2009*, which traces the descendants of Revolutionary War Captain John George Overmire and demonstrates the impact that one immigrant can have on the scope and breadth of American history.

A Revolutionary American Family: The McDonalds of Somerset County, New Jersey is Overmire's second major genealogical study in hardcover book form. It uncovers the fascinating story of some of the very first McDonalds to set foot in America, emigrants from an ancient Celtic tradition who established homes for themselves in the colonial East New Jersey wilderness, joined in the struggle for independence, fought alongside George Washington and helped to shape America's destiny.

The McDonalds of Lansingburgh, Rensselaer County, New York: The Pioneering Family of Richard and Catharine (Lansing) McDonald and Their Descendants is a supplement to the earlier McDonald book containing the history of this heretofore-lost line of descendants of Maj. Richard McDonald of Somerset County.

Overmire's extensive work on the American Overmyers and the McDonalds of Somerset County has made him the world's leading authority on those ancestral lines of research.

History is the story of us all. Each one of us has a story worth telling. Overmire reminds us that greatness lies not only in those who are celebrated on the monumental stages of the world, but also in the quiet, unseen passing of ordinary human beings, those who live their lives with courage and determination to meet the everyday challenges that ultimately move us all further down the path toward a better community, a stronger nation and a kinder, more responsible world.